Creative Tensions

Creative Tensions

An Introduction to Seventeenth-Century French Literature

Nicholas Hammond

Duckworth

First published in 1997 by
Gerald Duckworth & Co. Ltd.
The Old Piano Factory
48 Hoxton Square, London N1 6PB
Tel: 0171 729 5986
Fax: 0171 729 0015

A catalogue record for this book is available
from the British Library

ISBN 0 7156 2801 1

Typeset by Ray Davies
Printed in Great Britain by
Redwood Books Ltd, Trowbridge

Contents

Contents

Illustrations between pages 22 and 23

Acknowledgements

It is difficult not to be enticed by the vitality and inventiveness of French texts from the seventeenth century. My own enthusiasm for the period has been greatly augmented by the interest shown by students and colleagues. The idea for this book came from a series of undergraduate lectures which I gave in 1995 and 1996 at Cambridge University, and I am grateful to all those who attended and commented on the original lectures.

I would like to thank in particular the following people who have provided active support and help in the production of this book: Peter Bayley, Russell Goulbourne, Richard Parish, Jeremy Robbins and Judy Sproxton. Robin Baird-Smith and Martin Rynja at Duckworth have been an invaluable source of encouragement and assistance. I am indebted also to the generosity of Gonville and Caius College, Cambridge, for material assistance.

Author's Note

Detailed bibliographical references have been kept to a minimum in this book. Lists of secondary reading appear at the end of each chapter. Page or line numbers have been given only to works which are widely available in modern editions. All references to theatre written in verse are made in the order of act, scene, line number: e.g. I, 3, 549. Plays written in prose are referred to solely by act and/or scene number. Reference to other prose writings is made according to genre: e.g. by chapter number, maxim number, date of letter etc. Short isolated pieces (such as individual poems, portraits and conversations) are mentioned only by their title or genre. All translations of French quotations are my own.

Preface

The seventeenth century is an age which has justly been celebrated for its many towering literary figures. The names Corneille, Racine and Molière, for instance, are associated with a golden age of theatre in France which has never been surpassed. The plays of all three playwrights are still to be seen regularly on the French stage, and performances in English translation of Corneille and Molière in particular have been especially popular. La Fontaine's *Fables* are still read and enjoyed by children and adults of many nationalities. Moreover, the modern novel is widely thought to have emanated from seventeenth-century prose fiction, as encapsulated in the psychological intricacies of Mme de Lafayette's *La Princesse de Clèves*. In the field of philosophy and thought, we find such famous names as Pascal and Descartes, both of whom had enormous impact in and beyond France. Descartes, in his espousal of the importance of human reason, is acknowledged as the originator of modern philosophy. Pascal, whose work in scientific and mathematical fields has given his name to such diverse aspects as a unit of pressure, a triangle and even a computer language, is no less influential as a commentator on the human condition, pertaining not only to the society of his day but to all subsequent societies, as has been shown by his great popularity in successive centuries. The French *moralistes*, such as La Rochefoucauld and La Bruyère, are known for their profound insight into the complexities of humans and their interaction within society. Today, thinkers are still engaging with questions raised by many of these writers.

Women writers in the seventeeth century achieved a prominence hitherto unattained. Owing to the establishment of salons dominated by women, where groups discussed such issues as the equal education of men and women and even the tyranny of marriage, many new writers emerged, most notably Mme de Lafayette and Madeleine de Scudéry. Another woman writer who is still read widely, Mme de Sévigné, did not even intend to publish her correspondence. But her letters are still admired for their elegance, wit and beautifully crafted style. For the reason that she embraces so much of the spirit and exuberance of the seventeenth century, I have chosen both to end this preface and to conclude the book with her. In a letter to her daughter, dated 14 July 1680, she encapsulates the excitement of the age explaining that her writing is 'un torrent retenu que je ne puis arrêter' (a suppressed torrent that I cannot hold back).

I

Rules and Terms

When we look back at an age or period, there often exists the temptation to categorize it, to wrap it up into a neat package which will keep it safe from becoming too difficult or complicated to understand. In French literature, the century which seems to have suffered most from this convenient packaging is the seventeenth century. Usually when this period is evoked, people mention the rules and conventions, probably thereby implying that the litera-ture emanating from it must be at best stiff and formal and at worst boring. Moreover, words like 'baroque' (for the earlier part of the century) and 'classicism' (for the later part) are used, as if all literature of the period must fit into one or the other category.

As with most stereotypes, there is often an element of truth in them, but they tend to simplify and distort the real issues. The liveliness and sense of experimentation which inform so many texts from the seventeenth century are inevitably ignored. In this chapter, I shall consider some of these stereotypes of seven-teenth-century literature, with particular reference to a number of well-known works, in order to try and show how it is the creative tensions within these works which make them remarkable, not the rules to which they may seem to subscribe. Initially, a few general remarks about the purpose of this book are needed.

The primary aim of the book is to offer a brief but (I hope) suitably tantalizing taste of the richness of literary material from the seventeenth century. However, it is not intended as a detailed comprehensive survey of all seventeenth-century French literature. There are several guides, listed in the bibliography at the end of each chapter, which provide both a general background to the period and an overview of the literature.

Nor do I intend to concentrate exclusively on individual writers, although many of the best known literary figures of the day will be discussed and included in the Glossary at the end of the book. Again, many studies on separate authors exist. As useful as these kinds of study undoubtedly are, certain key aspects of the period are either excluded or over-simplified. My aim is to focus more closely on the complexities and conflicts within writings of the time. Through an examination of the creative tensions which are generated by those conflicts, a fuller picture of the age can emerge from the stereotype of inflexibility.

But first, a closer consideration of some of those stereotypes is necessary.

1. Rules

There are many possible explanations as to why the seventeenth century in France has been perceived as a period of rigid rules and conventions. Two major factors stand out, one academic, the other political, although inevitably the two overlap: the founding of the Académie française in 1635, and the accession to the throne of Louis XIV in 1643.

The Académie française

The Académie started originally as a group of literary friends who met at the house of Valentin Conrart, Louis XIII's secretary, to discuss the works which they were writing. Cardinal Richelieu heard of the meetings and decided to make them a symbol of national prestige, granting them his official protection at the beginning of 1635. The members formed their own constitution and received the official approbation of the king.

The primary objective of the Académie was to purify the French language and to maintain linguistic and literary standards for the nation. On the linguistic side, one major project culminated in the publication in 1694 of the *Dictionnaire de l'Académie française*. Although bilingual dictionaries, such as Nicot's Latin-French *Trésor de la langue française* (1606) and Cotgrave's French-English dictionary (1611), existed already, this constituted the first monolingual dictionary project. Because of the long gestation of the undertaking, two other monolingual dictionaries appeared before the publication of the Académie dictionary, Richelet's *Dictionnaire français* (1680) and Furetière's *Dictionnaire universel* (1690). These three works played a significant role in the standardization of both spelling and the choice of what was considered to be appropriate vocabulary.

A major participant in the preparation of the Académie's new dictionary was Claude Vaugelas, who presented his own *Remarques sur la langue française* (1647) to the Académie. In his work, he discusses what he considers to be the correct use of the French language, drawing examples from the French court and contemporary authors. His aim consisted primarily in attaining clarity through the use of language which he saw as governed by reason.

This idea of the rational basis of language derived in many ways from the affirmation by René Descartes (1596-1650), who is generally regarded as one of the principal originators of modern philosophy and science, at the beginning of his *Discours de la méthode* (1637): 'le bon sens est la chose du monde la mieux partagée' (good sense is the most widely shared thing in the world). Other writers who were influenced by Descartes sought to banish obscurity from their use of language. Antoine Arnauld and Pierre Nicole, in their *Logique* (1662), for example, went even further, asserting that 'le meilleur moyen pour éviter la confusion des mots [...] est de faire une nouvelle langue' (I.xii.86) (the best way to avoid the confused meaning of words is to construct a new language).

However, as fundamental as this overarching concern for the clarity of language was to many writings of the seventeenth century, it does not take into account the important role which the obscurity of language played in works from the period. One writer,

Blaise Pascal (1623-1662), who was closely connected to the circles which both Arnauld and Nicole frequented, claimed in his *Pensées* (published posthumously in 1670) that reason itself is 'ployable' (flexible) and therefore corruptible. The ambiguity of language became for Pascal an important sign of human weakness, displaying each person's inability to attain true clarity by him or herself.

On the literary side, one of the Académie's principal functions was to dictate matters of style and convention. The controversy which was provoked by the appearance of Corneille's play *Le Cid* in 1637 provided the Académie with its first test. Objections to the play revolved around the fact that Corneille had not adhered closely enough to the three unities of time (all the action of the play must take place within the space of 24 hours), place (all the events should occur in one place) and action (there should only be one central plot). As a result, the Académie commissioned one of its members, Jean Chapelain, to write a report entitled *Sentiments de l'Académie sur le Cid*. To a large extent, this debate brought to the fore the question of whether rules and regulations should be applied to drama and was instrumental in leaving the impression to later generations that literature from the period was inherently inflexible and artificial. I shall discuss this controversy at greater length in Chapter 2.

However, it should be remembered that at the same time that playwrights and theorists were arguing over the rules of theatre, so too were they discussing the necessity to make the theatre psychologically convincing. The term which they used, *vraisemblance*, means literally 'seeming true', but is best translated as 'probability'. In order for the tragic effect of the play to be felt by the audience, all elements should be probable. Significantly, the playwright who would seem to conform most closely to the rules and unities of the theatre, Jean Racine, was the one to advocate most enthusiastically the need for *vraisemblance*. As he wrote in the preface to his play *Bérénice* (1670), 'il n'y a que le vraisemblable qui touche dans la tragédie' (in tragedy, only the probable moves the audience). Moreover, even within the rigid application of rules, tensions are found: for example, even though Racine adhered closely to the three unities, this did not mean an unquestioning use of them. Many of his central characters would appear to be struggling on a social, moral and theatrical level against the very constraints which are imposed on them. In *Andromaque* (1667), at a crucial point in the drama, the character Hermione within one twelve-syllable line (alexandrine) seems to throw into question the three unities of place, action and time: 'Où suis-je? Qu'ai-je fait? Que dois-je faire encore?' (V, I, 1393) (Where am I? What have I done? What am I still to do?).

Prose writing by contrast seemed not to conform to any existing rules. Indeed, many prose works of the central years of the century, such as Sorel's *Berger extravagant* (1627-8), Scarron's *Roman comique* (1651-7) and Furetière's *Roman bourgeois* (1666), seem as much concerned with the act of writing itself and experimentation as with telling a story.

Louis XIV

The figure of Louis XIV is central to the seventeenth century, both for the length of his reign and the mythology which surrounded his persona. He succeeded to the throne at the age of four in 1643 and reigned for 72 years until his death in 1715. Protected initially by cardinal Mazarin, after the deaths of the immensely powerful cardinal Richelieu in 1642 and Louis XIII in 1643, it was during this royal reign that the cult of 'Gloire' (Glory) came to the fore and that rules governing people's lives and their response to the King were imposed. All media (fine art, coins, medals, theatre, music, opera) were directed towards the glorification of Louis. Comparisons were frequently made to the great age of ancient classical times, and grand names, such as 'Le Roi Soleil' (the Sun King), were applied to the monarch.

But underneath the propaganda of Louis XIV's reign, tensions can again be found. On a political level, the objection to the fiscal powers of the royal government led to the period of civil unrest

(1648-1653) known as the Fronde. On a literary level, amongst all the works praising the King, Peter Burke lists in his book, *The Fabrication of Louis XIV*, some 70 works (mostly published anonymously) explicitly denouncing the overbearing authority of Louis XIV. Even works which on the surface pay lip-service to the King contain tensions which are not immediately apparent. In the theatre, playwrights were particularly concerned to lavish praise upon the King, for, faced with the continuing opposition of the Church to the theatre (see Chapter 3, and for tensions within the Church itself, Chapter 4), they depended on Louis XIV's good will. Yet, this fact did not preclude covert criticism of the monarch. At the end of the comic playwright Molière's *Amphitryon* (1668), for example, it is left to the servant Sosie to question the notion of authority (in this case that of the god Jupiter), where it would seem that any liberty can be taken by those in power: 'Le seigneur Jupiter sait dorer la pilule' (III, 10, 1913) (Lord Jupiter certainly knows how to sugar the pill). It is worth considering the conclusion of another Molière play, *Tartuffe* (1669), for it both appears to offer unquestioning praise of the King and has often been criticized as typical of the inflexibility and implausibility of seventeenth-century dénouements. At the end of the play, just as the villain Tartuffe seems to have succeeded in evicting Orgon and his family from their home, the King's representative turns the tables on Tartuffe and pardons Orgon for his misdemeanours, thus showing the monarch's true goodness.

> **L'Exempt:** Remettez-vous, monsieur, d'une alarme si chaude.
> Nous vivons sous un prince ennemi de la fraude,
> Un prince dont les yeux se font jour dans les coeurs,
> Et que ne peut tromper tout l'art des imposteurs.
> D'un fin discernement sa grande âme pourvue
> Sur les choses toujours jette une droite vue;
> Chez elle jamais rien ne surprend trop d'accès,
> Et sa ferme raison ne tombe en nul excès.
> Il donne aux gens de bien une gloire immortelle;
> Mais sans aveuglement il fait briller ce zèle,

Et l'amour pour les vrais ne ferme point son coeur
A tout ce que les faux doivent donner d'horreur.
Celui-ci n'était pas pour le pouvoir surprendre,
Et de pièges plus fins on le voit se défendre.
D'abord il a percé, par ses vives clartés,
Des replis de son coeur toutes les lâchetés.
Venant vous accuser, il s'est trahi lui-même,
Et, par un juste trait de l'équité suprême,
S'est découvert au prince un fourbe renommé,
Dont sous un autre nom il était informé;
Et c'est un long détail d'actions toutes noires
Dont on pourrait former des volumes d'histoires.
Ce monarque, en un mot, a vers vous détesté
Sa lâche ingratitude et sa déloyauté;
A ses autres horreurs il a joint cette suite,
Et ne m'a jusqu'ici soumis à sa conduite
Que pour voir l'impudence aller jusques au bout,
Et vous faire, par lui, faire raison de tout.
Oui, de tous vos papiers, dont il se dit le maître,
Il veut qu'entre vos mains je dépouille le traître.
D'un souverain pouvoir, il brise les liens
Du contrat qui lui fait un don de tous vos biens,
Et vous pardonne enfin cette offense secrète
Où vous a d'un ami fait tomber la retraite;
Et c'est le prix qu'il donne au zèle qu'autrefois
On vous vit témoigner en appuyant ses droits,
Pour montrer que son coeur sait, quand moins on y pense,
D'une bonne action verser la récompense;
Que jamais le mérite avec lui ne perd rien;
Et que, mieux que du mal, il se souvient du bien.

Dorine: Que le ciel soit loué!

Madame Pernelle: Maintenant je respire.

Elmire: Favorable succès!

Mariane: Qui l'aurait osé dire?

Orgon (à Tartuffe): Hé bien! te voilà, traître …

Cléante: Ah! mon frère, arrêtez.

(V, 7, 1905-96)

(Officer: Do not be so alarmed, sir. We live under the rule of a prince who is the enemy of fraud, a prince who can see into our hearts and whom all the guile of impostors cannot deceive. The keen discernment of that great mind makes him see everyting in the correct perspective. Nothing can surprise him and his constant reason never leads him to excess. He bestows immortal glory on people of worth; but he is not blind in making this great zeal shine forth: his love for the good and true does not make him close his mind to a sense of horror at those who are false. He could not have been caught out by this man, and he has been seen escaping much more subtle traps than this. From the outset he clearly discerned all the cowardice of his heart. Coming to accuse you, Tartuffe betrayed himself, and in full justice unmasked himself before the king to be a known scoundrel, whose other activities were already known by the king. The long list of his dark deeds could fill several volumes. In short, this Monarch was full of hatred for this man's ingratitude and disloyalty towards you. He put me under Tartuffe's orders only to see the lengths to which he would take his impudence and so in so doing to exonerate you. Yes, all your papers which he says he has in his possession and which must betray you, by an act of sovereign power his Majesty breaks the contract which bound you to give him all your worldly goods and pardons you for that secret offence in which the escape of your friend involved you; This is the prize which the King bestows on you for the former loyal service which you were seen to offer him; in order to show that he can reward a good service when you least expect it, that merit is important to him and that he remembers good more than bad.

Dorine: Heaven be praised!

Madame Pernelle: Now I can breathe again.

Elmire: What a favourable result!

Mariane: Who would have thought it?

Orgon: Now I'll show you, traitor ...

Cléante: Stop, brother.)

The dominant interpretation of the Exempt's speech, followed by the other characters' joy, must be that the King has seen through the malicious ways of Tartuffe and that goodness has triumphed over evil. Yet, if we consider the speech and its aftermath more carefully, the words might be seen to contain tensions which are not immediately apparent. First, the verb most often attached to the King in the Exempt's speech is 'voir' (to see). He is an all-seeing monarch (line 1910) and a monarch who is seen (line 1918). In other words, he is both spectator and actor. The function of his authority resides primarily in its theatricality. Second, the reaction of the other characters should be taken into account. The expression of pious joy after the speech, 'Que le ciel soit loué' (Heaven be praised!), can be read as ironic, because it is spoken by the character least concerned with religious behaviour, the servant Dorine. Moreover, the spontaneity of the reaction of the four characters who speak immediately after the speech is undermined by the fact that the alexandrine is rigidly divided between the speakers into 6 syllables each. They could be seen simply to be expressing relief in a self-consciously mechanical way. Significantly, the father of the household, Orgon, fails to praise the King and is only intent on exacting revenge on Tartuffe. All these factors point to tensions beneath the surface which are as crucial as the panegyric of the King. The King, for example, is praised for his intervention, but this could simply be read as a publicity stunt, designed to display his goodness to his people. Theatricality in this sense might have a negative value, yet, as we shall see in the course of this book, images of the theatre and theatricality permeate much of seventeenth-century France, often as a positive force. Moreover, the King's performance (through the character of the Exempt) in *Tartuffe* is only one of many: Tartuffe himself is playing a role (deemed to be hypocritical), but so too is Orgon's own wife Elmire, who plays the part of wishing to be seduced by Tartuffe so that he may be unmasked (viewed positively by the eventual outcome of Tartuffe's arrest). Similarly, the characters' joy at the end of the play can be interpreted as genuine, but the continuing obsessiveness of Orgon and the irony of Dorine's holy words act as a counterpoint to the prevailing happiness.

It is my aim in this book, therefore, to look for these kinds of tension, for under the exterior of order in seventeenth-century

French writings many conflicting tensions both energize and deepen the structured and seemingly simple surface.

2. Terms

The notion of order has permeated most terminology used to describe the seventeenth century. As I mentioned at the beginning of this chapter, two terms in particular, 'baroque' and 'classicism', have been used to summarize respectively the early and the later years of the century and are often seen to be exclusive of each other. Writing in the 1960s, the critic Jean Rousset captures well both the conventional meaning of the two terms and the tension within them:

> On dit: ordre, mesure, raison, règle, et c'est le classicisme. On dira donc: désordre, outrance, fantaisie, liberté, et ce sera le baroque. Cosmos et chaos; équilibre et jaillissement vital. C'est vrai et c'est faux.
>
>   'Le Baroque et le Classicisme', in *French Classicism: a critical miscellany*, ed. J. Brody (Englewood Cliffs, 1966), p. 158.
>
> (It is said: order, measure, reason, rule, and that is classicism. It will therefore be said: disorder, excess, fantasy, freedom, and that will be the baroque. Cosmos and chaos; balance and lively outpouring. It is both true and false.)

Within this scheme, baroque denotes disorder and energy, characterized, for example, by Pierre Corneille's early comedies, whereas classicism is epitomized by order and regulation, as found in the first successful tragedies of Pierre Corneille and the tragedies of Racine. As Rousset implies, however true these appellations may seem, inevitably they over-simplify any text under consideration. Corneille's early comedies may indeed be dominated by fantasy and a lack of structure, but this does not prevent them from containing elements which are highly ordered and seemingly 'classical'. *L'Illusion comique* (first performed in 1636), for example, as its title suggests, plays upon the illusory nature of the theatre, described by Corneille himself as 'une galanterie extravagante' (an extravagant collection of intrigues). Yet the three central acts form its own self-enclosed entity, where, as Corneille accentuates, 'le succès en est tragique' (its outcome is tragic). Similarly, although Racine's tragedies exemplify restraint and order, modelled closely on classical sources, Racine can still introduce characters into traditional legends which played no role in the original versions (such as Eriphile in *Iphigénie*, 1674) and takes pains to adapt his material to suit the requirements of the age in which he is writing.

The label 'classicism' communicates most obviously the importance attached in the seventeenth century to imitation of the ancient Classical world. Indeed, I shall return in this book to the significance of borrowing from and interpretation of Roman and Greek texts. Yet, as we shall see in the chapter on genre (Chapter 6), although genres such as the theatre and heroic poetry were dominated by classical models, other genres were less obviously related to the ancient Romans and Greeks. On another level, the heroic myth and espousal of patriarchal values (typified by Louis XIV as Father of the State) point to seventeenth-century writers' perception of ancient times, but again, as I shall discuss in Chapter 7 on gender, there were many opposing forces to the heterosexual male-dominated world of the day.

One important debate in the seventeenth century which is closely related to these tensions is worth singling out.

The Querelle des anciens et des modernes

The adherence of many writers to tradition formed the basis of an ongoing argument in the second half of the century with those who favoured the establishment of a distinctively modern French culture. This continuing debate was known as the *Querelle des anciens et des modernes* (Quarrel of the ancients and moderns). No single chapter will be devoted to this *querelle*, because so many issues which underpin my discussion throughout this book are informed by the contrasting interpretions of ancient authorities.

Prominent amongst the supporters of the *ancien* cause were Nicolas Boileau, the satirist and author of *L'Art poétique* (1674), in which he espouses the need for simplicity and clarity, Racine, and the *moraliste* Jean de La Bruyère, all of whom we shall encounter in the course of this book. Major players in the *moderne* camp were Charles Perrault, now best known for his fairy-tales, whose *Parallèle des anciens et des modernes* (1688-97) provoked much controversy, and Bernard le Bovier de Fontenelle, who asserted in his *Digressions sur les anciens et les modernes* (1688) that intellectual progress inevitably made *modernes* surpass *anciens* in scientific matters.

Not only, therefore, are the terms 'baroque' and 'classicism' inadequate to describe fully the complexity of the seventeenth century, but the terms themselves are too slippery for simple classification. They might be useful on a superficial level, but they offer the all too easy temptation to sum up the seventeenth century in two words. I shall attempt to resist such temptation in the course of this book. We shall see in Chapter 5 how two other notoriously difficult terms, *honnêteté* and *préciosité*, escape simplistic definition.

To conclude this chapter, it is worth reconsidering some elements of what I have discussed already, but through a different perspective: two paintings by the French seventeenth-century artist, Nicolas Poussin (1594-1665). Both pieces display a sense of structure, which only on closer examination reveal conflict.

Les Cendres de Phocion (1648)

The first impression of the composition as a whole is that of a huge ordered landscape. In the centre a sturdy temple, symbolizing rules, order, authority and religion, dominates the picture. In front of the temple, on the fields, and bathed in light, people seem to be enjoying their existence, leading untroubled and ordered lives. But in the foreground, partly in shadow, partly in sunlight, a woman is

Les Cendres de Phocion by Nicolas Poussin.
From Liverpool, Walker Art Gallery, National Museums and Galleries on Merseyside.

Paysage avec un homme tué par un serpent by Nicolas Poussin.
The National Gallery of Art, London.

kneeling, burying the ashes of her dead husband. On one level, it is a loving, natural act, celebrating the passage of time. On another level, however, the fact remains that her husband, Phocion, an Athenian general, has been refused burial by the authorities. Anybody who tries to bury him will be sentenced to death. His widow is therefore risking her own life in defying the regulations. The fear and tension generated by this subversive act is mirrored in the figure of the widow's confidant, who is standing in the shadows and turned away in fear. Even more sinister, hidden amongst the trees on the right, a spy lurks. Beneath the ordered surface of the painting, inner tensions are palpable.

Paysage avec un homme tué par un serpent (1648)

As in *Les Cendres de Phocion*, the general perspective is of an ordered and peaceful landscape. The boatmen continue on their daily business. But two figures in the foreground register both terror and surprise. The woman on the bank has been startled by the running man. However, she cannot see why he is frightened. In the shadows, in the foreground again, a pale body is encircled by a huge black snake.

The kind of oppositions that we find in these two paintings can be applied to many writings of the seventeenth century. The issues which have been raised briefly in this chapter will be developed during the course of the book. The overbearing sense of order (or temples in the sunlight) will not be ignored, but I shall examine the equally important role of disorder (the snake in the shadows). By considering both the overarching structure and the underlying tensions of various debates, we should reach a fuller understanding of a period which is often fascinating, occasionally frustrating, and always challenging.

Selected Reading

Reference

A. Adam, *Histoire de la littérature française du XVIIe siècle*, 5 volumes (Paris, 1962-8). Still the most comprehensive and detailed general survey of all aspects of seventeenth-century literature.

The New Oxford Companion to Literature in French, ed. Peter France (Oxford, 1995). This is an excellent introduction to all aspects of French literature (not simply the seventeenth century). Useful for brief summaries of writers, political and other key figures.

General (in English)

R. Briggs, *Early Modern France 1560-1715* (Oxford, 1977). A useful historical overview of the period.

J. Cruickshank, *French Literature and its Background 2: the seventeenth century* (Oxford, 1969). Although in some respects outmoded, it still provides very helpful background material to the seventeenth century.

W.D. Howarth, *Life and Letters in France: the seventeenth century* (London, 1965). A good general study.

D.C. Potts, D.G. Charlton, *French Thought Since 1600* (London, 1974). More specifically related to French philosophy, but the section on the seventeenth century is invaluable.

H. Stone, *The Classical Model: literature and knowledge in seventeenth-century France* (Cornell, 1996). A detailed analysis of experimentation in seventeenth-century France.

General (in French)

F. Gaiffe, *L'Envers du Grand Siècle* (Paris, 1924). A pioneering work in which the seventeenth century is reassessed through the analysis of manuscripts which do not form part of the traditional canon.

Littérature française du XVIIe siècle, ed. R. Zuber, L. Picciola, D. Lopez, E. Bury (Paris, 1992). An intelligent overview, dealing particularly well with questions of genre.

Louis XIV

P. Burke, *The Fabrication of Louis XIV* (New Haven and London, 1992). A very readable book on the image-making surrounding Louis XIV.

2

Tensions in Drama I

In seventeenth-century France, the theatre achieved a prominence which in many ways eclipsed other art-forms of the time. Indeed, knowledge of literature of the age has become synonymous with its great dramatists, Pierre Corneille, Molière and Racine. The active encouragement of first cardinal Richelieu and then Louis XIV gave the theatre a political and national importance which inevitably added to its prestige but which also obliged it to follow rigorous criteria. Those who were seen not to be conforming to the rules provoked controversy, which was exacerbated by the fact that the popularity of the theatre made each successive scandal public property. In fact, the many literary arguments which abounded in France at that time furnished the literate public with the same kind of prurient enjoyment that tabloid newspapers provide today.

The political pressure exerted by the all-seeing gaze of the monarch was not the only constraining force in the theatre at the time. The hallowed name of the Ancient Greek writer, Aristotle, was widely invoked. His *Poetics* in particular was regarded as the essential hand-book to the staging and writing of drama, and generally theorists and dramatists alike did not dare contradict his words. Many of the so-called 'rules' which were supposed to govern seventeenth-century drama emanated from Aristotle. As we shall see, the differing interpretations of Aristotle's pronouncements on the theatre formed the basis of a number of debates on the theatre.

Although there were many far-ranging discussions on the function of drama in the seventeenth century, I shall consider in this chapter three particular controversies which in many ways exemplify the way in which drama was changing in the course of the century. The first, that surrounding Corneille's *Le Cid*, can be linked to the evolution of tragedy in France. The second concerns Molière and the notion of comedy. The third relates back to Corneille and the quarrel of his supporters with a significant theorist of the time, the abbé d'Aubignac. The first two quarrels have been widely documented, as can be seen in the bibliography at the end of the chapter. The third is less well known but marks an important point in the development of dramatic theory and practice in the second half of the seventeenth century.

1. *Le Cid*

As I mentioned in the first chapter, the performance in 1637 of *Le Cid* came at particularly important time, soon after the creation of the Académie française. The controversy which the first performances and publication of the play provoked provided the Académie with its first major literary debate.

When Georges Scudéry published a strongly worded attack on Corneille in his *Observations sur le Cid* (1637), Guez de Balzac, who is remembered chiefly for his attempts to impose order and regularity in prose style, replied with a vigorous defence of Corneille. The highly publicized squabbles which then ensued resulted in Jean Chapelain, one of the founding members of the Académie, being commissioned to write a report entitled *Sentiments de l'Académie sur le Cid* (1637). In addition to these contributions, a number of jealous playwrights, most notably Jean Mairet, put their oars into the debate.

The objections to *Le Cid* were wide-ranging, but they can perhaps be classified under two categories: morality and the breaking of rules.

Morality

Critics of *Le Cid* were shocked by aspects which they deemed to be immoral. Indeed, Chapelain in his *Sentiments de l'Académie sur le Cid* stressed that certain immoral scenes, even if historically true, should be suppressed 'pour le bien de la société' (for the good of society). The major moral objection to Corneiile was that it was thought to be impossible for a man (Rodrigue) to marry or even to see a woman (Chimène) whose father he had just killed.

Rules

It was widely felt also that Corneille had paid insufficient attention to the rules of staging drama, as found in the *Poetics*. There was no unity of action; too many episodes (such as the Infanta's love for the character Don Rodrigue, which was seen by critics as peripheral to the plot) complicated the simplicity of the action. The lack of unity of place was also criticized, as four different locations, known as *multiple décor*, were used in the play. Although unity of time (all the action occurring within 24 hours) was observed, this was considered 'invraisemblable' (improbable), as too much occurred within that time (amongst other actions, two duels and a battle) for it to be plausible.

Also, the exact status of the play was unclear. It was initially labelled 'tragicomédie' (probably referring to the fact that the ending was not bloody) in 1637, but, perhaps partly in response to objections and partly in order to reflect changing tastes, as tragi-comedies as a genre became less popular after the 1630s, it was renamed 'tragédie' in the new edition of 1648.

As a result of the controversy, Corneille was to conform more closely to the unities in his next plays, *Horace* and *Cinna*, but Corneille was one of very few playwrights who, in his theoretical writings on the theatre, both paid lip-service to Aristotle and dared to contradict him. We shall see later how allegiance to Aristotle became a bone of contention between him and D'Aubignac.

Although *Le Cid* was attacked from many sides, Corneille was not slow to point out to his critics that the public flocked to see his plays. This was a useful weapon which Molière also was to use. Because of the public success of both Corneille and Molière's plays, criticism by other dramatists could easily be interpreted as sour grapes on their part.

2. *L'Ecole des femmes*

Like *Le Cid* for Corneille, *L'Ecole des femmes* was Molière's first major success. The storm of protest which greeted the first performances can also be compared to Corneille, for the play was deemed to be both immoral and opposed to the rules, this time of comedy.

On the moral level, the play was considered too full of sexual innuendoes. As far as rules were concerned, although Molière's use of unified action in the play conformed to Aristotelian definitions of drama, the general orthodoxy was that different types of comedy could not be combined in one play. *La belle comédie*, as higher forms of comedy were termed, should not coexist with farce. One critic of *L'Ecole des femmes*, Robinet, defined *la belle comédie* thus:

> où l'on remarque de beaux sentiments, où l'on voit des moralités judicieusement répandues, où, enfin, l'on trouve de quoi ces pièces qui sont des tableaux des passions, galamment touchés, s'instruire et se divertir agréablement.

> (where one can note fine sentiments and where one can observe judiciously disseminated morality, where one finds these plays to be gallantly treated depictions of the passions, from which one can both learn and be entertained.)

Farce belonged, so these critics thought, in a different context. At the time that Molière was writing, farce was performed by the Italian theatre troupe, based in Paris, and he was greatly influenced by them. *Commedia dell'arte*, as this form of comedy was called, placed emphasis on physical action. Various stock characters

(known as *zanni*) were used, and most wore masks, thus accentuat-
ing situation rather than characterization. Also, actors were generally not governed by a script but relied rather on improvised scenes
(*lazzi*).

Molière's innovation rested precisely in his ability to combine
both kinds of comedy. Therefore, if we take the first act of *L'Ecole
des femmes* as an example, the first scene consists of a conversation
between Arnolphe and Chrysalde, where the comedy is primarily
verbal. The twelve syllable alexandrine line is mostly unbroken,
and the speeches tend to be extended. Scene 2, on the other hand
– our first meeting with the servants Alain and Georgette – is
entirely based on the physical comedy of *commedia dell'arte*. A sense
of improvisation is communicated through the frequent repetition
of short phrases such as 'Vas-y, toi' (you go) and 'Ouvre' (Open up).
Although the text is technically written in alexandrines with rhym-
ing couplets, each line is broken up between different speakers,
adding pace and giving the language a prosaic quality. Whereas
the dominant vocabulary in scene 1 tends to be elevated, with
sophisticated word play (such as on the words 'sot' and 'sage' in
lines 82-3), literary reference (to Rabelais's *Tiers livre* in line 118)
and terms such as 'honnêteté' and 'appas', the vocabulary of scene
2 is both more direct and onomatopoeic, such as Arnolphe's call
'Holà ho' (line 204). The third scene reverts to comedy of language,
where Arnolphe revels in Agnès's innocence and perceives himself
to be master of the situation both verbally and in action.

Whereas the debate surrounding *Le Cid* prompted Corneille to
write tragedies which conformed more closely to the rules, the
criticism that *L'Ecole des femmes* did not follow the rules of comedy
inspired Molière to respond to his critics through the medium he
knew best, the theatre. His two metatheatrical excursions, *La
Critique de l'Ecole des femmes* and *L'Impromptu de Versailles* (both 1663),
are plays within plays where the characters discuss the nature and
purpose of comedy. In few ways are they innovative, as the first half
of the seventeenth century had seen a number of plays which were
self-reflective, notably Corneille's *Illusion comique* (1635) and Ro-

trou's *Le Véritable saint Genest* (1645). But they spell out a rejection of the need to be constrained by rules. In the *Critique*, for example, the response of the character Dorante to the pedant Lysidas's continual reference to Greek terms effectively satirizes those theorists who attempted to apply prescriptive rules to the theatre:

> Ah! monsieur Lysidas, vous nous assommez avec vos grands mots. Ne paraissez point si savant, de grâce. Humanisez votre discours, et parlez pour être entendu. Pensez-vous qu'un nom grec donne plus de poids à vos raisons?
>
> Act 6
>
> (Oh M. Lysidas, you are boring us with your long words. Please do not appear so learned. Make your speech more human, and speak in order to be understood. Do you think that a Greek word adds weight to your arguments?)

The stance taken by Dorante is intentionally anti-intellectual. Critics in the past have rather too readily assumed that the voice of Dorante is that of Molière himself. Although there may be points in common between the two, it should be remembered that Dorante is as much a creation as any other character. Molière himself was widely read (the Latin playwrights Plautus and Terence, for example, influenced his writing), and Dorante's anti-intellectual stance suits the purposes of this particular context. Rather than engaging in sterile debate, Molière therefore transforms the tensions of the conflict into theatrical format. He was certainly not averse to self-referentiality (as can be seen in the character 'Molière' in *L'Impromptu de Versailles* and the reference to himself in his final play, *Le Malade imaginaire*), but above all his plays are nourished on a notion of their own theatricality, as we saw for example in my discussion in Chapter 1 of the conclusion of *Tartuffe*. But above all, as Corneille did with his critics, Molière was able to remind his detractors of the fact that his plays were popular with audiences. To quote Dorante again in the *Critique*:

Je dis bien que le grand art est de plaire, et que cette comédie ayant
plu à ceux pour qui elle est faite, je trouve que c'est assez pour elle,
et qu'elle doit peu se soucier du reste.

Act 6

(I hold that the greatest art is to please; and once this play has
pleased those for whom it was written, I find that quite sufficient,
and it should not be concerned with other considerations.)

After all, one of the pedant Lysidas's principal objections to *L'Ecole
des femmes* is that it is 'trop comique' (too comical) and that all the
excesses of the character of Arnolphe 'font rire tout le monde'
(make everybody laugh).

3. Corneille and D'Aubignac

A similar claim could be made for the comic potential of the debate
between D'Aubignac and supporters of Corneille. The personal
insults which flew, particularly in the latter stages of the quarrel,
make for entertaining reading. But, more seriously, the debate
came at a significant point in the development of theatre in seventeenth-century France. I shall focus on three works which are
instrumental to the debate, D'Aubignac's *Pratique du théâtre* (1657),
Pierre Corneille's *Discours* (1660), and D'Aubignac's four *Dissertations contre Corneille* (1663).

La Pratique du théâtre (1657)

D'Aubignac's *Pratique* is of great importance. First, it was the only
comprehensive treatise on the theatre from the time. Another
treatise from the century, La Ménardière's *Poétique* (1640), for
example, related mostly to the past, as it gave no contemporary
examples. Second, it was innovative, especially in D'Aubignac's
interpretation of the importance of the concept of *vraisemblance*.
Third, he drew almost all examples from the theatre of his time,
most notably Corneille himself. Fourth, he was less interested in

the moral importance of the theatre than in its impact on the spectator. In other words, as the title *Pratique* implies, he was concerned above all with practice rather than theory.

Corneille's Discours (1660)

The publication in 1660 of Corneille's three *Discours* ('De l'utilité et des partis du poème dramatique', 'De la tragédie et des moyens de la traiter selon le vraisemblable ou le nécessaire', and 'Des trois unités') and an *Examen* accompanying each of his plays published before that date was to mark the beginning of the antagonism between Corneille and D'Aubignac. Despite the fact that D'Aubignac had mentioned Corneille often and in a favourable light in his *Pratique*, Corneille did not repay the compliment to D'Aubignac in his *Discours*. Moreover, without mentioning D'Aubignac by name, he contradicted a number of D'Aubignac's assertions, most notably on the question of *vraisemblance* in the theatre. While D'Aubignac had stressed the Aristotelian notion that the subject matter of a play should above all be plausible, Corneille had gone so far as to say that this was 'une maxime très fausse' (a most erroneous maxim). D'Aubignac later prepared an edition of the *Pratique* (which never appeared), crossing out all references to Corneille.

Quatre dissertations contre Corneille (1663)

As a result of this snub, D'Aubignac set about writing a critique of some recent plays by Corneille. The first *dissertation* was directed against *Sophonisbe* (first published by Corneille earlier in 1663), the second against *Sertorius* (1662) and the third against *Oedipe* (1659). All three display interesting developments on his remarks in the *Pratique*. As in the earlier work, at all times he mentions the effect which the plays have on spectators, ever mindful of how the theatre works in practice. It is in this respect that D'Aubignac is similar to Corneille, Molière and Racine. Quite apart from becoming en-slaved to rules, all four are careful to accentuate the primary importance of the theatrical effectiveness of plays. As Racine states in the preface to *Bérénice*, 'la principale règle est de plaire et de toucher' (the principal rule is to please and move).

In the *Dissertations*, D'Aubignac's main criticism of Corneille's recent plays resides in the fact that they are not successful as theatre (a view subsequently justified by the relative obscurity of these later Corneille plays compared to his early successes). In the second *dissertation*, for example, D'Aubignac complains about the over-abundance of sub-plots (which he calls 'polymythie') in *Sertorius*, which make the play too complex for the spectator to digest:

> Cette Polymythie nous prive encore d'un plus grand plaisir, en ce qu'elle ôte à M. Corneille le moyen de faire paraître les sentiments et les passions, c'est son fort, c'est son beau, et c'est ce qu'on ne trouve pas en ce Poème. Il ne l'a pas fait, parce qu'il ne s'est pas mis en état de le pouvoir faire; aussi le confesse-t-il lui-même dans la Préface que cette Pièce n'a point ces agréments qui sont en possession de faire réussir au Théâtre les Poèmes de cette nature. Il lui faut tant de temps pour expliquer les intérêts et les desseins de ses personnages, qu'il en reste fort peu pour mettre au jour les mouvements de leur coeur.
>
> *Dissertations*, p. 35

> (This Polymythia deprives us of a still greater pleasure, in that it prevents M Corneille from allowing emotions and passions to appear, the real strength and beauty of his plays, certainly not to be found in this play. He did not achieve this, because he did not allow himself the means to achieve it; consequently he confesses himself in the Preface that this play has none of the entertaining aspects which can make plays of this kind succeed in the theatre. He needs so much time to explain the interests and designs of his characters that there is very little room to bring the inner workings of their hearts to light.)

In the third essay, on *Oedipe*, D'Aubignac returns to the theme of *vraisemblance* and choice of subject-matter, criticizing Corneille's decision to portray the story of Oedipus's murder of his father, even if historically true, as inappropriate for the stage:

> ... dès lors que l'on n'est pas convaincu de la vraisemblance des événements, tout y languit et tout y déplaît. Et quand même l'histoire nous fournirait des exemples certains de ces actes de cruauté, ils ne seraient pas plus vraisemblables ni meilleurs à mettre sur la Scène. Toutes les choses vraies ne sont pas vraisemblables, je crois que M. Corneille en sera d'accord avec Aristote qui le dit, et avec la raison qui ne se peut contredire.
>
> p. 84
>
> (... when one is not convinced by the plausibility of the events, everything becomes dull and displeasing. And although history might provide strong examples of these acts of cruelty, this would not make them any better or more plausible to stage. All true things are not plausible; I think that M Corneille will agree with those words by Aristotle, as they are expressed with a line of argument which cannot be contradicted.)

The significance of this debate is all the more striking when we consider that at the time of this particular *querelle*, Racine was just embarking upon his career as a dramatist. *La Thébaïde*, his first play, was completed at the end of 1663. It is probable that Racine followed this debate closely. First, we know that he possessed a copy of D'Aubignac's *Pratique du théâtre*, and second, he seems to have assimilated all of D'Aubignac's criticisms (especially concerning unity of place and *vraisemblance*) of Corneille. In so doing, he was able to distance himself from Corneille and conform to theoretical thinking of the time.

D'Aubignac's fourth essay consists mostly of personal attacks against Corneille and self-defence against the counter-polemic which Donneau de Visé (1638-1710) had written anonymously in support of Corneille. In addition to commenting on the plays themselves, De Visé launched a series of barbs against D'Aubignac, mostly about his age, failing memory and lack of success as a dramatist. D'Aubignac repaid the compliment, pretending that

Corneille was the author of the counter-polemic, and lambasting him for his famous meanness and pomposity. Reference is even made to Corneille's sudden decision to give himself the aristocratic title M. de Corneille and to Molière's satire in *L'Ecole des femmes* of Corneille's younger brother's assumption of the title Sieur de l'Isle. D'Aubignac accuses Corneille of attempting to ban Molière's *L'Ecole des femmes* when it had first appeared the year before.

*

I have chosen to concentrate on these tensions within drama, because they show that the theatre of the day did not constitute a series of inflexible plays which obeyed all the laws. Indeed, the very success of Corneille and Molière in particular seems to lie in the fact that they did not obey all regulations. It should not be forgotten that the theatre thrived on these controversies. The more public the squabbles, the more likely the plays would succeed at the box-office. In many ways, dramatists found themselves caught between their claim that the art of pleasing the audience was their primary concern and the need to answer to the accepted conventions. For this reason, Corneille admits at the beginning of his first *discours* that some of his plays have not conformed closely enough to the rules:

> Bien que, selon Aristote, le seul but de la poésie dramatique soit de plaire aux spectateurs, et que la plupart de ces poèmes leur ayent plu, je veux bien avouer toutefois que beaucoup d'entr'eux n'ont pas atteint le but de l'art [...]; et pour trouver ce plaisir qui lui est propre et le donner aux spectateurs, il faut suivre les préceptes de l'art, et leur plaire selon ses règles.
>
> *Oeuvres complètes* (Paris, 1963), ed. J. Stegman, p. 821

> (Although, as Aristotle mentions, the sole aim of dramatic poetry is to please the spectators, and although most of my plays have succeeded in pleasing them, I must still confess that many of them have not achieved this aim; in order to attain the appropriate

pleasure and give it to the spectators, one must follow the precepts
of art and please the audience according to its rules.)

Many theorists or self-appointed arbiters of theatrical fashion, such
as Chapelain and D'Aubignac himself, tried their own hand at
writing plays which obeyed all the rules, with noticeably poor
results. A throw-away remark by Condé, a major patron of the arts
in the seventeenth century, about D'Aubignac's failure as a dramatist uncovers a more profound point about the successful dramatists
of the age. Tensions rather than rules give the plays their appeal
and their depth:

> Je sais bon gré à M. d'Aubignac d'avoir si bien suivi les règles
> d'Aristote: mais je ne pardonne point aux règles d'Aristote, d'avoir
> fait faire une si méchante tragédie à M. d'Aubignac.
>
> (I am grateful to M d'Aubignac for having followed Aristotle's rules:
> but I cannot forgive Aristotle's rules for having made M d'Aubignac
> write such a terrible tragedy.)

The tension between obeying rules and writing successful drama
permeates much of the seventeenth century. On the one hand,
successful playwrights were keen to keep to the formula which
contributed to their popularity. On the other hand, because they
were so successful, they were forced to defend themselves before
the authorities of the day.

    In the next chapter, I shall consider a more fundamental threat:
those authorities who objected morally to the theatre as an institution, and the problem amongst the dramatists themselves of trying
to prove the moral usefulness of their plays.

Selected Reading

H.T. Barnwell, *The Tragic Drama of Corneille and Racine* (Oxford, 1982). A
well-informed discussion of many central issues concerning the two
major tragic dramatists of the seventeenth century.

A. Calder, *Molière: the theory and practice of comedy* (London, 1993). A workmanlike but thorough analysis of Molière's theatre.

D. Clarke, *Pierre Corneille* (Cambridge, 1992). A good analysis of the political dimension of Corneille's earlier plays.

P. Corneille, *Writings on the Theatre*, ed. H.T. Barnwell (Oxford, 1965). An edition of Corneille's theoretical writings (in the original French), with useful notes in English.

G. Couton, *La Vieillesse de Corneille* (Paris, 1948). In French, invaluable for detailed analysis of the dispute between D'Aubignac and Corneille.

D'Aubignac, *Dissertations contre Corneille*, ed. N. Hammond and M. Hawcroft (Exeter, 1995). Introduction, notes and text in French. The complete text of D'Aubignac's polemical pieces against Corneille, together with general background information.

W. Howarth, *Molière: a playwright and his audience* (Cambridge, 1982). Excellent on the context of Molière's theatre.

Tensions in Drama II

Although, as we saw in the last chapter, the theatre reached a peak of popularity in the seventeenth century, it was only as late as 1641 that Louis XIII published an edict absolving actors from the charge of infamy. Before that date, actors and playwrights inevitably felt threatened and were obliged to justify the value of their work. The conclusion of a play like *L'Illusion comique*, first performed in 1636 and published in 1639, which constitutes a plea for understanding of the theatre, is shown to be all the more significant when we realize the climate in which it was written.

> **Pridamant:** J'ai cru la comédie au point où je l'ai vue,
> J'en ignorais l'éclat, l'utilité, l'appas
> Et la blâmais ainsi, ne la connaissant pas.
>
> V, 5, 1674-6

(I considered the theatre at face value and was unaware of its lustre, usefulness and attraction, and so I blamed it, not fully knowing it.)

As a result of the relaxation of rules concerning actors and the theatre, for the first time a permanent theatre of largely secular inspiration performed throughout 1639. Both cardinal Richelieu and Louis XIV, when he assumed full power, actively supported the theatre. As we have seen, the theatre became enshrined within the notion of authority, with the Académie française making official pronouncements on the aims and rules of drama. Moreover, Louis XIV was personally responsible for the founding of the Comédie-Française in 1680. The Comédie, an institution which still survives, was formed by the fusion of the Hôtel de Bourgogne and the Théâtre de Guénégaud, and as a national theatre retained the exclusive rights to perform plays in French. Having the support of both Richelieu and Louis XIV proved to be a very useful weapon in the armoury of those who sought to defend the theatre against its continuing detractors. Samuel Chappuzeau, for example, whom I shall discuss more fully later, mentions these two men as two principal reasons why the theatre should be supported, in his work, *Le Théâtre français*, of 1674:

> ... que le grand Cardinal de Richelieu, l'un des plus éclairés de tous les hommes, l'aimait, l'appuyait, honorait les auteurs de son estime, favorisait les comédiens; et, pour dire plus que tout cela, que le roi, l'invincible Louis, les délices de ses peuples et l'admiration de l'univers, trouve des charmes dans la comédie, dont il connaît parfaitement toutes les beautés, et qu'il la prend pour un de ses plus doux divertissements, quand il se veut donner quelques moments de relâche dans les grands soins qui l'occupent incessamment pour la gloire de son règne et le bien de ses sujets.
>
> *Livre* I, p. 27

> (... the great cardinal Richelieu, one of the most enlightened of men, loved and supported it [the theatre], honoured and respected authors and favoured actors; and, what is more, the invincible King Louis, delight of his peoples and wonder of the universe, finds great charm in the theatre, knowing perfectly as he does all its beauty; it serves as one of his most delightful diversions, when he wishes to relax momentarily from the great cares which occupy him ceaselessly for the continued glory of his reign and the greater good of his subjects.)

Unfortunately for Chappuzeau, only a few years after he published *Le Théâtre français*, Louis XIV adopted a pious image in the 1680s. Most particularly after his marriage in 1683 to Mme de Maintenon, renowned for her religious devotion, Louis XIV was persuaded to withdraw his active interest in the theatre, which returned the country to a climate of intolerance. In 1685, the Edict of Nantes (dating from 1598), which had allowed both Protestants and Catholics to practise their faith freely and openly, was revoked and Racine retired from the theatre between 1677 and 1689.

However, throughout the century, whether the theatre was officially recognized or not, there continued to rage a debate about its purpose. La Bruyère best captures the contradictions and tensions of the age in *Les Caractères* (first published in 1688) when he compares the seventeenth-century theatre to the differing attitudes of the Ancient Greeks and Romans:

> La condition des comédiens était infâme chez les Romains et honorable chez les Grecs: qu'est-elle chez nous? On pense d'eux comme les Romains, on vit avec eux comme les Grecs.
>
> *Des jugements*, no. 15

(The acting profession was dishonourable for the Romans and honourable for the Greeks: how is it for us? We think of actors like the Romans, but we live with them like the Greeks.)

In this chapter I shall focus on two aspects of these tensions of drama, first the moral objections (mostly of the Church) to the theatre as an institution, second the need for dramatists to defend the moral usefulness of the theatre.

1. Moral Objections to the Theatre

Church vs Theatre

There are many reasons why the Church was hostile to the theatre, and I shall consider some of these later in this chapter. But above all, it must be remembered that the resurgence of the theatres represented a significant threat to what might crudely be termed the Church's box-office appeal. The power of the pulpit was undeniable. Priests were proud of their ability to sway the hearts of their congregation through the combination of powerful rhetoric, spectacle and music. Mme de Sévigné, for example, makes it very clear in letters to her daughter that she enjoys hearing père Bourdaloue's sermons primarily for their dramatic effect. There were even hand-books available which gave advice on how best to preach a sermon. Michel Le Faucheur, for example, wrote a work, first published in 1657 and soon reprinted (indicating its success), entitled *Traité de l'action de l'orateur ou de la prononciation et du geste* (Treatise on the orator's delivery or on pronunciation and gestures), in which he is at pains to stress its use for preachers:

> Mon but est seulement de leur apprendre à parler en sorte, qu'au lieu de rebuter leurs auditeurs par une prononciation vicieuse, et par un geste mal-seant, ils servent à leur édification, non seulement par leur discours; mais encore, autant qu'il se peut, par la bienséance qu'ils garderont en leur prononciation et leur geste.
>
> 1667 edition, pp. 21-2

> (My sole aim is to teach them to speak as appropriate to their status, so that, instead of putting off their listeners by terrible pronunciation or an inappropriate gesture, their listeners may be edified not only by their speech but, as much as possible, by the decorum which they will maintain in their pronunciation and gestures.)

Other writers from the seventeenth century had seen very clearly how theatrical the art of preaching was. In La Bruyère's *Caractères*, for example, he makes just such a connection between preaching and the theatre, criticizing preachers for having become too theatrical:

> Le discours chrétien est devenu un spectacle. Cette tristesse évangélique qui en est l'âme ne s'y remarque plus: elle est suppléée par les avantages de la mine, par les inflexions de la voix, par la régularité du geste, par le choix des mots, et par les longues énumérations.
>
> *De la chaire*, XV, 1

> (The sermon has become a spectacle. That evangelical gravity which is its soul is no longer to be found: it is replaced instead by the advantages of physical appearance, by vocal inflections, by regular gestures, by choice of words, and by long enumerations.)

On the one hand, as La Bruyère points out, the serious art of speaking in church can become too influenced by a sense of drama. But on the other, skilful presentation plays a large part in keeping the congregation's attention. An earlier writer, Pascal, noticed precisely this need for preachers to give an effective performance in order to persuade and sway the imagination of their audience. In the fragment from the *Pensées* devoted to imagination, he notes those trivial aspects which undermine the effectiveness of a preacher:

> Que le prédicateur vienne à paraître, si la nature lui a donné une voix enrouée et un tour de visage bizarre, que son barbier l'ait mal rasé, si le hasard l'a encore barbouillé de surcroît, quelque grandes vérités qu'il annonce je parie la perte de la gravité de notre sénateur.
>
> Lafuma edition, 44

> (Think of a preacher appearing: if nature has given him a hoarse voice and a strange-looking face, if his barber has shaved him badly and if moreover he turns out to be grubby, whatever great truths he may be pronouncing, I wager the loss of gravity of the [listening] senator.)

It is therefore not surprising that the Church felt threatened by the theatre (with its very own brands of brilliant rhetoric, spectacle, music, costumes, and actors). As the Church saw it, those connected with the theatre stood a very good chance of winning over souls to their decidedly secular ranks.

Theatre as a Pernicious Influence: Nicole and Chappuzeau

Those theologians who objected to the theatre often supported their argument by referring to Church Fathers such as St Augustine who, they insisted, condemned the theatre. Countering them, defenders of the theatre claimed that Augustine was referring to a completely different kind of theatre from that which they had in the seventeenth century. In the *Epître* to his play *Théodore*

(1646), for example, which he labels a 'Tragédie Chrétienne' (Christian Tragedy) and which deals with the martyrdom of a saint, Corneille makes this point forcefully:

> ... j'oserai bien dire que ce n'est pas contre des comédies pareilles aux nôtres que déclame saint Augustin, et que ceux que le scrupule ou le caprice ou le zèle en rend opiniâtrement ennemis, n'ont pas grande raison de s'appuyer de son autorité. C'est avec justice qu'il condamne celles de son temps, qui ne méritaient que trop le nom qu'il leur donne de spectacles de turpitude, mais c'est avec injustice qu'on veut étendre cette condamnation jusqu'à celles du nôtre, qui ne contiennent pour l'ordinaire que des exemples d'innocence, de vertu et de piété.

> (... I will even dare to say that St Augustine is not speaking against plays like ours, and that those whose moral scruples or capriciousness or zeal make them obstinate enemies of the theatre do not have good reason to rely on his authority. It is just that he condemns those plays of his time and calls them spectacles of depravity, but it is unjust to extend this condemnation to the plays of our time, which for the most part contain examples only of innocence, virtue and piety.)

As we saw in Chapter 2, the ancient authorities were as often argued about as they were used as moral exemples.

In order to show the extreme positions which different sides took in the debate over the theatre, I have chosen to give sustained examples of one vigorous defender from each side, Pierre Nicole and Samuel Chappuzeau. Although they were not in direct confrontation with each other, they each encapsulate some of the major arguments used by those who opposed and those who supported the theatre.

Nicole's *Traité de la comédie*, first published in 1667, is one of many pieces condemning the theatre which appeared in the second half of the seventeenth century. One such work, Conti's *Traité de la comédie et des spectacles* (1666), contains a theme common to most anti-theatre tracts of the time, that the theatre encourages unnatu-

ral passions: 'le but de la Comedie est d'esmouvoir les passions,[...]: et au contraire, tout le but de la Religion Chrestienne
est de les calmer, de les abbattre et de les destruire autant qu'on
peut en cette vie' (the goal of the theatre is to provoke passions; on
the contrary, the whole goal of the Christian Religion is to calm,
beat down and destroy those passions as much as can be done in
this life). Voisin, in his *Défense du traité de Monseigneur le prince de Conti
touchant la comédie et les spectacles* (1671), develops this point: according to him, illicit passions on stage are always accompanied 'd'une
image de grandeur, et de générosité'. (by an image of greatness and
nobility). Divided into ten short chapters, Nicole's *Traité* moves
from an attempt to explain those reasons which are offered by
people who justify the theatre to a condemnation of the theatre and
all actors, with a description of the vices which they provoke,
concluding with a depiction of the ways in which the theatre
contradicts the Christian way of life. Chappuzeau, on the other
hand, was keen to emphasize both the usefulness and stature of the
theatre. In the following figure, I have placed comments by Nicole
and Chappuzeau side by side in order to show the ways in which
each party treats similar questions.

P. Nicole, *Traité de la comédie*

S. Chappuzeau, *Le Théâtre français*

i.a: Il est impossible de con-
sidérer le métier de Comédien,
et le comparer avec les devoirs
du Christianisme, sans reconnaître
qu'il n'y a rien de plus indigne d'un
enfant de Dieu et d'un membre de
Jésus-Christ, que cet emploi. (Ch. II)

i.b: Quoique la profession des
comédiens les oblige de représenter incessamment des intrigues
d'amour, de rire et de folâtrer sur le
théâtre, de retour chez eux ce ne
sont plus les mêmes; c'est un grand
sérieux et un entretien solide; et
dans la conduite de leurs familles
on découvre la même vertu et la
même honnêteté que dans les familles des autres bourgeois qui
vivent bien. (*Livre* III)

(It is impossible to consider the acting profession and compare it to the duties of Christianity without recognizing that there is nothing more unworthy of a child of God and Christ's family than this job.)

(Although actors' work obliges them to act out incessantly love intrigues, to laugh and frolic on the stage, when they return home they are no longer the same; an actor is both serious and speaks solidly; in the conduct of their families, the same virtue and politeness as other correct-living bourgeois families can be seen.)

ii.a: La Comédie éloigne tous les remèdes qui peuvent empêcher la mauvaise impression qu'elle fait. Le coeur y est amolli par le plaisir. L'esprit est tout occupé des objets extérieurs, et entièrement enivré des folies que l'on y voit représenter. (Ch. IV)

ii.b: Elle [la Comédie] n'a rien de sale, si le poète ne sort des bornes que la bienséance lui prescrit, et ce n'est proprement que contre les spectacles ou sanglants, ou déshonnêtes, qui combattent la charité et la pureté du christianisme, que les conciles et les Pères se sont déclarés. (*Livre* I)

(The theatre banishes all remedies which can prevent the bad impression that it makes. The heart is softened by pleasure. The mind is occupied by external objects and is completely inebriated with the madness which is seen performed there.)

(It has nothing filthy about it if the dramatist does not leave the boundaries which propriety prescribes. It is only against bloody or improper spectacles opposing the charity and purity of Christianity that the Councils and holy Fathers have declared themselves.)

iii.a: Non seulement les Comédies et les Romans rendent l'esprit mal disposé pour toutes les actions de Religion et de piété, mais il en conçoit du dégoût pour toutes les actions sérieuses et communes. (Ch. VIII)

iii.b: Ceux qui voudraient absolument l'interdire comme une chose qui ne regarde pas directement le salut seraient obligés d'en retrancher une infinité de cette nature, où il aurait plus à redire qu'à la comédie, et que l'on souffre aisément. (*Livre* I)

(Not only do plays and romances make the mind ill disposed towards all acts of religion and piety, but the mind also feels disgust for all serious and ordinary acts.)

(Those people who would like to prohibit it completely because it does not directly concern salvation should be obliged to suppress an infinite number of the same kind, where there is more to be answered for than in the theatre, but which is happily endured.)

iv.a: Le besoin que l'on a de se délasser quelquefois, ne peut donc aussi excuser ceux qui prennent la Comédie pour un divertissement, puisqu'elle imprime ... de mauvaises qualités dans l'esprit, qu'elle excite les passions, et qu'elle y dérègle toute l'âme. (Ch. VIII)

iv.b: ... s'il faut aujourd'hui détourner les yeux de toutes les choses vaines, il ne faut pas aller ni à la cour ni au cours, deux superbes spectacles. (*Livre* I)

(One's occasional need to relax cannot excuse those who take the theatre as a diversion, for it imprints bad things on the mind, excites the passions and throws one's whole soul into disorder.)

(... if today we must avert our eyes from all vain things, we ought not to go to court or to the hunt, both of which are great spectacles.)

v.a: ... si toutes les choses temporelles ne sont que des figures et des ombres, en quel rang doit-on mettre les Comédies qui ne sont que les ombres des ombres ...? (Ch. X)

v.b: ... la comédie a été en tres grande estime dans toute l'antiquité; que les Grecs et les Romains ... en ont également reconnu l'utilité. (*Livre* I)

(... if all temporal things are but figures and shadows, on what level should one put plays which are nothing other than shadows of shadows.)

(... the theatre was held in great esteem throughout antiquity; both the Greeks and Romans recognized its usefulness.)

In **i.a**, Nicole's uncompromising condemnation of the very profession of acting might seem unduly harsh, even for the seventeenth century. Yet it should be remembered that actors were often refused Christian burial. Molière, for example, was only allowed a Christian burial in 1673 after the King had intervened to make a special case for him. It is therefore not surprising that Chappuzeau should emphasize that, whatever the frivolity of the roles which actors may play, in their ordinary lives they were as virtuous as any other person (**i.b**). As for the experience of the theatre, Nicole claims (**ii.a, iii.a** and **iv.a**) that inevitably spectators will be corrupted by such external pleasures and that these pleasures will deter them from serious thought. Chappuzeau, on the other hand, stresses that, as long as certain boundaries are maintained, the theatre cannot be harmful. Using a similar argument to Corneille, he claims that the theatre which was condemned by the Church Fathers (such as Augustine) was entirely different from that of their day (**ii.b**). Moreover, the accusations made against the theatre could easily be extended to many other diversions (**iii.b**), including those amusements, as Chappuzeau is clever to underline, held most dear by the royal family (**iv.b**). Whereas Nicole tries to show the ephemerality of the theatre (**v.a**), Chappuzeau is at pains to show its long history (**v.b**).

2. Theatre as Moral Instruction

Theorists

In order to counter the accusations of the anti-theatre lobby, playwrights and theorists alike were forced to rethink their strategy. By stressing the moral dimension of drama, they hoped at least to prove that the theatre had a useful role to play in society. The leading figures in the *querelle* surrounding *Le Cid* were quick to mention this idea of moral usefulness. Scudéry (in his *Observations sur Le Cid*) spoke of the need for drama to teach 'l'horreur du vice, et l'amour de la vertu' (the horror of vice and love of virtue). Chapelain (the Académie's official arbiter over the affair) saw 'l'utilité' (usefulness) as being the main aim of the theatre. And La Ménardière, whose *Poétique* (1640) I mentioned in Chapter 2, thought that tragedy could only achieve its aim 'par l'utile exposition des Vertus récompensées, et des vices châtiés' (through the useful exhibition of virtue rewarded and vices punished). Perhaps not surprisingly, Corneille (who, as we have seen, was at the receiving end of many of these criticisms of so-called 'immoral' theatre) was less keen to toe the party line. Indeed, he emphasizes that no distinction should be made between virtue and criminality in so far as they are theatrically appropriate. In this way, he writes in his *Discours du poème dramatique* of 'le caractère brillant et élevé d'une habitude vertueuse ou criminelle, selon qu'elle est propre et convenable à la personne qu'on introduit' (the brilliant and elevated character of a virtuous or criminal state of mind, as long as it is particular to or conforms to the person who is being introduced). Racine in his prefaces tends not to write of moral usefulness. It was only in the Preface to *Phèdre* (his final play before abandoning secular theatre) and in his two religious tragedies that he began to mention such issues, declaring in the Preface to *Esther* (written for the school-girls of the Saint-Cyr convent), for example, that he had been careful to avoid the mingling of sacred and profane subjects, thereby avoiding the 'impressions dangereuses' which profane matters can provoke in every innocent convent girl. Laclos's *Les Liaisons dangereuses* (published almost a century later in 1782), in which the convent girl Cécile is corrupted by the manipulative Valmont and Mme de Merteuil, would seem to fulfil such dire predictions!

Example of Tartuffe

Whereas neither Corneille nor Racine's plays were threatened with immediate closure because of their content, Molière faced a far greater test. The Church thought that his *Tartuffe* represented a direct attack on the priestly profession, and the first version of the play was very quickly banned. Molière therefore had the choice of either accepting the prohibition or trying to defend the moral status of his play. Unsurprisingly he chose the latter path. With the benefit of hindsight, it is easy to support Molière against his critics. After all, his name has survived in public consciousness and theirs have not. Therefore, when he states in the Preface to *Tartuffe*,

> J'ai mis tout l'art et tous les soins qu'il m'a été possible pour bien distinguer le personnage de l'hypocrite d'avec celui du vrai dévot.
>
> (I have employed all possible art and care to clearly distinguish the figure of the hypocrite from that of the truly devout person.)

we are inclined to believe him. But it is worth noting that Molière wrote this preface after the play had been banned and for a later version. Our reading of his statement of moral intent should be coloured by a realization of the pragmatic needs of the situation. If we consider his words more closely, in conjunction with the Premier Placet (the introduction) which he wrote before the first performance of the first version, further questions are raised. He claims in the Preface to make a clear distinction within the play between the true and false *dévot*. Clearly Tartuffe himself is the incarnation of the falsely pious man. But who is the true devout person with whom Molière claims to have contrasted Tartuffe? Orgon's brother-in-law, Cléante, makes a speech (itself an addition to the later 1669 version) in Act I, scene 5, about the need to distinguish between true piety and hypocrisy, but his concerns seem above all to be humanist ones and not those of Christian piety. At no point does he show himself to be an orthodox Christian. Of the other major characters, Dorine the servant, Elmire (Orgon's wife) and Damis (Orgon's son) show no interest in devotion. In fact, the only two characters who, although blinkered and misled by Tartuffe, could be seen to be truly religious and surely sincere in their beliefs are Orgon and his mother, Mme Pernelle. The question remains whether they can be considered as serious representatives of true devotion. In the Premier Placet (of 1664), Molière's tone is very different from that in the later Preface: 'je n'avais rien de mieux à faire que d'attaquer par des peintures ridicules les vices de mon siècle' (there was nothing better for me than to attack through ridiculous portrayals the vices of my century). For the most part, those characters in *Tartuffe* who are depicted as 'ridicules' are the very characters who are sincere in their devotion, Orgon and Mme Pernelle. Tartuffe himself could be interpreted as insinuating, even sinister, but rarely ridiculous. Even in Act 4, when he is caught attempting to seduce Elmire, he is out-ridiculed by Orgon whose slowness in emerging from his hiding-place is the main source of our mockery. The sincerity of Molière's assertion that he has made every effort to distinguish between true devotion and hypocrisy is therefore somewhat doubtful.

What then might Molière's principal target of satire be? Could his detractors be correct in thinking that he was attacking the Church? A good clue to Molière's original intentions might well be found in the original sub-title of the play. Initially, he entitled it 'ou l'hypocrite' (1664), changing it later to 'ou l'imposteur' (1667). The essential difference between a hypocrite and an impostor is that a hypocrite is an insider (like a lascivious priest who within the Church preaches sexual virtue), whereas an impostor is an outsider who plays a role of something which he is not (such as a lay-person pretending to be a priest). Both the first sub-title and contemporary accounts of Tartuffe's (or Panulphe as Tartuffe was originally called) dress suggest that Tartuffe was originally conceived as an insider of the Church rather than an outsider. I shall return shortly to the possible reasons for Molière's hostility towards the church.

In Chapter 2, I discussed three controversies surrounding the theatre. The prohibition of *Tartuffe* provoked its very own *querelle*, with a number of pamphlets in support and in condemnation of the play. The most prominent piece written in its support was the anonymous *Lettre sur la comédie de l'imposteur* (1667), variously claimed to have been written, amongst others, by Molière himself, Donneau de Visé and La Mothe le Vayer. The *Lettre* is divided into two sections, the first giving a detailed description of the 1667 version of the play and the second offering a defense of its moral value. The letter is eloquent, especially in its definition of the ridiculous: 'si le Ridicule consiste dans quelque disconvenance, il s'ensuit que tout mensonge, déguisement, fourberie, dissimulation, toute apparence différente du fond, enfin toute contrariété entre actions qui procèdent d'un même principe, est essentiellement ridicule' (if the ridiculous consists of some kind of disparity, it follows that every lie, disguise, deceit, dissimulation, every appearance which is different from the inner being, in fact every contrast between actions which proceed from the same principle, is essentially ridiculous). Nonetheless, as in the Preface to *Tartuffe*, it was necessary for the moral content of the play to be emphasized by its defenders so that official permission could be received for its restoration to the public stage.

Some defenders of Molière's moral uprightness saw in *Dom Juan* (1665), which he wrote immediately after the first version of *Tartuffe*, an appropriately moral tale. After all, the philandering, sinning protagonist receives his just deserts at the end and is sent into the flames of hell. However, there are many signs which dictate against such a reading. First, the character of Dom Juan is surely attractive; that is why he has managed so often to escape from difficult situations. As a character, he has managed to persuade and seduce all those around him. Similarly, as a figure on the stage, he should be attractive to the audience. Recent research has equated him with traditional trickster figures from legends such as Brer or Peter Rabbit. These tricksters are mischievous but ultimately likeable. Second, the ending of the play (by itself terrifying and appropriately admonishing) is immediately deflated by Sganarelle's request for his wages. Any seriousness which we might have read in the dénouement is transformed into laughter. Third, if we look closely at what exactly sends Dom Juan to his doom, questions arise. If we consider the sermons which exist from the seventeenth century (notably those by Bossuet and Bourdaloue), the sins which are most railed against are all those which Dom Juan commits: sensuality, polygamy, failure to repay debts, blasphemy and lack of charity. But, each time that he commits one of these sins which were so frowned upon by the religious authorities of the day, he succeeds in getting away, just as Brer Rabbit always gets away with his crimes. Crucially, only one crime sends Dom Juan directly to his doom, and it is a crime not mentioned so much in seventeenth-century sermons as the central theme of *Tartuffe*, hypocrisy. Dom Juan pretends in front of his father to have become converted, to be a truly religious man (Act 5, scene 1). In other words, he has become a religious hypocrite, like Tartuffe. Only then is he led off to his fate. It is as if Molière sees the worst sin as that of religious hypocrisy. It is not known what precisely led to *Dom Juan* being withdrawn abruptly, despite a very successful first few performances, but once more the Church could understandably have seen itself as threatened by the play.

The reasons, then, for Molière's hostility to the Church are clear. As we have seen in the first half of this chapter, actors' and playwrights' livelihoods were threatened by the opposition of the Church to the theatre.

In the last chapter, we saw how Molière managed to transform the tensions of the debate about the purpose of drama (and specifically comedy) into *La Critique de l'Ecole des femmes* and *L'Impromptu de Versailles*. Similarly, but perhaps even more forcefully, we have seen in this chapter how the tensions between theatre and Church were transmuted into two of his best known plays, *Tartuffe* and *Dom Juan*. Although the discussions about the moral usefulness of drama and the opposition of the Church often proved to be constraining forces in the theatre, so too did the tensions of the time lead to be a positive creative force. The rules may have been important, but the working within or against the limits were even more significant. In the next chapter, I shall consider tensions which existed in the Church itself.

Selected Reading

C. Bourqui, *Polémique et stratégies dans le Dom Juan de Molière* (Paris-Seattle, Tübingen, 1992). Excellent for the connection between the play and

4

Tensions in Religion

In the last two chapters, we have seen the extent to which the theatre felt it necessary to respond to or react against the worlds of politics and the Church. In this chapter, I shall consider how tensions within the Church were themselves closely connected to political matters. One outstanding figure who was involved in debates both within the Church itself and the battle between Christian apologists and sceptics was Blaise Pascal (1623-1662): he will form the central focus of this chapter.

A major event which still had repercussions in seventeenth-century France was the Council of Trent (1545-63), where the Catholic Church attempted to respond to the rise of Protestantism by reforming and defining its doctrines. Although one of the intentions of the Council had been to remove various types of abuse within the Church, the hardening of its stance against the Protestant Church and the fact that papal power was strengthened considerably proved to be more significant. There then resulted in France the rise of gallicanism, the name given to the various movements which asserted the independence of the French Church over Rome. Gallicanism existed both within the judicial sphere of secular France, where the king was given authority to appoint archbishops and bishops within France, and in the Church itself, where bishops demanded autonomy from the king and the pope in their dioceses. Many bishops who were known as Jansenists attached themselves strongly to this idea of autonomy, relying ever more on the contemplative life and on conscience, thus

setting themselves apart from the Jesuits, who stressed allegiance to
the central authority of Rome.

Notwithstanding the fact that the Edict of Nantes, which ended
the French wars of religion and which allowed the Protestant
Huguenots free exercise of their religious faith, was retained between 1598 and 1685, there was still much religious tension
throughout the century. One continuing factor of the tension was
the presence of Protestantism. Another factor was the significant
dispute within the Catholic Church between the Jesuits and the
Jansenists. Pascal in his *Ecrits sur la grâce*, albeit from a very biased
angle, underlines the disparity in thought between Protestants
(named by him as *Calvinistes*), Jesuits (*Molinistes*) and Jansenists
(*Disciples de saint Augustin*):

Calvinistes

L'opinion des Calvinistes est:

Que Dieu, en créant les hommes, en a créé, les uns pour les
damner et les autres pour les sauver, par une volonté absolue et sans
prévision d'aucun mérite.

Que, pour exécuter cette volonté absolue, Dieu a fait pécher Adam,
et non seulement permis, mais causé sa perte.

Qu'il n'y a aucune différence en Dieu entre *faire* et *permettre*.

Que Dieu, ayant fait pécher Adam et tous les hommes en lui, il
a envoyé Jésus-Christ pour la rédemption de ceux qu'il a voulu
sauver en les créant et qu'il leur donne la charité et le salut indubi-
tablement.

[...]

Molinistes

En haine de cette opinion abominable et des excès qu'elle
enferme, les Molinistes ont pris un sentiment non seulement op-
posé, ce qui suffisait, mais absolument contraire. C'est que Dieu a
une volonté conditionnelle de sauver généralement tous les
hommes. Que pour cet effet Jésus-Christ s'est incarné pour les
racheter tous sans en excepter aucun, et que ses grâces étant
données à tous, il dépend de leur volonté et non de celle de Dieu,
d'en bien ou d'en mal user. [...]

Cette opinion, contraire à celle des Calvinistes, produit un effet tout contraire. Elle flatte le sens commun que l'autre blesse. Elle le flatte en le rendant maître de son salut ou de sa perte. Elle exclut de Dieu toute volonté absolue, et fait que le salut et la damnation procèdent de la volonté humaine, au lieu que dans celle de Calvin l'un et l'autre procèdent de la volonté divine.

[…]

Disciples de saint Augustin

Ils considèrent deux états dans la nature humaine:

L'un est celui auquel elle a été créée dans Adam, saine, sans tache, juste et droite, sortant des mains de Dieu, duquel rien ne peut partir que pur, saint et parfait;

L'autre est l'état où elle a été réduite par le péché et la révolte du premier homme, et par lequel elle est devenue souillée, abominable et détestable aux yeux de Dieu.

Dans l'état d'innocence, Dieu ne pouvait avec justice damner aucun des hommes, Dieu ne pouvait même leur refuser les grâces suffisantes pour leur salut.

Dans l'état de corruption, Dieu pouvait avec justice damner toute la masse entière; et ceux qui naissent encore aujourd'hui sans en être retirés par le baptême sont damnés et privés éternellement de la vision béatifique, ce qui est le plus grand des maux.

Suivant ces deux états si différents, ils forment deux sentiments différents touchant la volonté de Dieu pour le salut des hommes.

Lafuma edition, pp. 312-3

(*Calvinists*: The opinion of the Calvinists is: that God in creating men created some to be damned and others to be saved, through an absolute will and no provision for any merit; that, in order to carry out this absolute will, God made Adam sin, not only allowing but causing his fall. That there is no difference in God between *making* and *allowing*. That God, having made Adam and all men through him sin, sent Jesus Christ to redeem those whom he wanted to save when creating them, to whom he inevitably gives charity and salvation.

Molinists: in hatred for this abominable opinion and for its inherent excesses, the Molinists took a position which was not only opposed to it, which was warranted, but completely the opposite. They believe that God has a conditional will to save all men in general. That for this purpose Jesus Christ became incarnate to save everyone without exception, and as his grace is given to all, it depends on men's will, and not God's, to use well or badly as they see fit. This opinion, which contradicts that of the Calvinists, produces quite the opposite effect. It flatters common sense in a way that the opposing opinion casts it down. It flatters common sense, making it master of its own salvation or fall. It excludes all absolute will from God, and makes salvation and damnation proceed from human will, whereas in Calvin's view they both proceed from divine will.

Disciples of St Augustine: They consider two states in human nature: the one is that which was created in Adam, clean, without stain, just and upright, leaving God's hands from which nothing can leave other than pure, holy and perfect; the other is the state into which it was reduced by the sin and revolt of the first man, and through which it has become sullied, abominable and detestable in God's eyes. In their state of innocence, God could not with justice send any men to damnation, God could not even refuse them sufficient grace for their salvation. In their state of corruption, God could with justice send all of mankind to damnation, and also those who are still born today without being exempted through baptism are condemned and eternally deprived of the vision of beatitude, which is the greatest of all ills. Following these two very different states, they form two different sentiments concerning God's will for the salvation of men.)

Central to Pascal's discussion of these different denominations within the Church is the question of grace (the supernatural assistance of God bestowed upon human beings) and free will. From his position, whereas the Calvinists believe in predestination of those who will be saved and those to be damned, thereby allowing no room for human free will, the Jesuits by contrast appear to give little power to God and are over-generous with free will.

The term Jansenism was used by opponents to describe those figures associated with Port-Royal. Port-Royal comprised two convents, Port-Royal-des-Champs (eighteen miles south west of Paris), which was founded in 1204 but which only became a house of major importance after the appointment at the age of ten of Angélique Arnauld (1591-1661) as abbess in 1602, and Port-Royal de Paris (in the Faubourg Saint-Jacques), to which the community moved in 1625. In addition to the nuns, various men, known as the *solitaires*, the most prominent of whom was Angélique Arnauld's brother Antoine Arnauld (1612-1694), attached themselves to both Port-Royal and Port-Royal-des-Champs (which became a fully active house again in 1648). The Jansenists were named after the Flemish theologian Cornelius Jansen (1585-1638), bishop of Ypres from 1636. In his *Mars gallicus* (1635), Jansenius (as he was better known) explicitly denounced Richelieu's foreign policy, and to-gether with his friend, Jean Duvergier de Hauranne (1581-1643), the abbé de Saint-Cyran, criticized the *raison d'état* – Richelieu's doctrine of identification of State affairs with the Church. In the year that Jansenius died, 1638, Saint-Cyran was imprisoned by Richelieu, because he was considered a threat to the State. He was only released on the 6th February 1643, two months after the death of Richelieu, by Richelieu's successor, cardinal Mazarin. Saint-Cyran himself died shortly after his release. In the meantime, between 1638 and 1642, the Society of Jesus, a religious order founded in the sixteenth century, enjoyed unprecedented power of doctrine. Not only did they have the support of Richelieu, but since the reign of Henri IV, who died in 1610, there had been a tradition of Jesuits acting as spiritual confessors to the reigning monarch. Such domination inevitably led to abuse of power and subsequent attacks by other religious groups on the morality of the Jesuits. At this time, the rigorous and ascetic members of Port-Royal began to voice their objections.

In 1640, Jansenius's *Augustinus*, which contitutes a close reading of many writings of St Augustine, was published posthumously. The book became a significant focal point for those at Port-Royal. Their unbending Augustinianism pitted themselves directly against the less rigid doctrines of the Jesuits. In 1643, the year that Louis XIII died, *Augustinus* was condemned by the Inquisition and by Pope Urban VIII in a papal bull. In the same year, Antoine

Arnauld's *De la fréquente communion* was published, in which he pleaded for a return to the simplicity of Christianity. It was clear that he considered the Jesuits to have strayed from this simplicity in their obfuscation of many central Christian doctrines. Subsequently, five propositions allegedly taken from *Augustinus* were declared heretical by Pope Innocent X in 1653 and by Pope Alexander VII in 1656. The publication of Arnauld's *Lettre d'un docteur de Sorbonne à une personne de condition* in 1655 and a *Seconde lettre à un duc et pair* in 1656 only served to enflame the debate. Arnauld argued that, in the censure of these five propositions, one had to distinguish between *fait* – whether in fact these propositions were to be found at all in *Augustinus* – and *droit* – if they were to be found, were they even heretical? Later in 1656, the theologians at the Sorbonne met to consider Arnauld's comments. They decided to censure him first on his remarks about the *question de fait*. In their judgement, the five propositions had been taken directly from *Augustinus*. They then moved to an examination of the *question de droit*.

1. *Lettres Provinciales*

At this stage, it was clear that a defender of those at Port-Royal was badly needed. However, with the risk of imprisonment which they ran if they were discovered to be authors of an attack on the Jesuits, it was difficult to know who could safely champion their cause. Pascal turned out to be the ideal person. At that time he was famous only for his mathematical and scientific gifts and was certainly not known for polemical writings. If he published anonymous attacks on the Jesuits, therefore, it was much less likely that his identity would be revealed. Also, although he was sympathetic towards Port-Royal, he was not known for his links with them. Another major advantage was that, because he was not trained as a theologian, he would be able to write with a freshness and immediacy which would be appealing and understandable to a wider range of people, not simply to those interested in the complexities of the religious debate. This ploy succeeded, as the letters were indeed brought to the attention of the secular world, particularly that of the literary salons.

The letters were published anonymously, eighteen appearing at regular intervals between January 1656 and March 1657. A nineteenth letter was projected and partly written, but by then the terms of the debate had changed greatly, and the project was abandoned. When the letters were first collected in a single volume in 1657, for the first time the pseudonymous Louis de Montalte appeared as their author.

These letters exemplify the manifold religious tensions of the age in their vigorous defence of Port-Royal and their equally combative attack on the Jesuits. Moreover, they form part of an ongoing debate, as after the appearance of the third letter the Jesuits started writing their own counter-polemical pieces. In the later letters, clearly the speaker is defending himself against these attacks by the Jesuits.

The letters can be divided into two main groups: letters 1-10, where we find an interplay between a naïve persona (the speaker/writer of the letters, sometimes referred to by critics as Louis de Montalte), a Jansenist friend and some Jesuit priests; and letters 11-18, where all pretence of a 'real' exchange between different personae is dropped, and where the speaker (called the polemicist by some critics) is now much more knowing and attacks the Jesuits directly, becoming more specific in the final two letters.

Letters 1-10

Letters 1-3 constitute a last-minute attempt to save Arnauld from being condemned by the Sorbonne on the *question de droit*. Although this aim failed early on (Arnauld was officially censured in February 1656), it succeeded in bringing the central themes of the debate to the attention of a public previously not versed in complex theological argumentation. This was precisely a point used in the Jesuit counter-polemic, where one writer (somewhat condescendingly) accuses Montalte of exposing complicated arguments and works 'aux yeux des ignorants, et en langue vulgaire, et à des personnes qui ne peuvent discerner le faux d'avec le vrai, l'utile d'avec le dommageable, le recevable d'avec ce qui ne l'est pas' (to the eyes of ignorant people and in the French language, and to people who cannot distinguish between truth and falsity, between what is useful and what is harmful, and between what is allowed and what is not). The major aspects of Pascal's defence of Arnauld centre on terminology (such as the *question de droit* and the *question de fait*) and, most importantly, on the notion of grace. The Jesuits had invented a term called 'grâce suffisante' (sufficient grace), which, according to Pascal, gave themselves the power to 'play God' and absolve or neutralize the sins of their followers. This contrasts strongly with the Jansenists' more orthodox belief in 'grâce efficace' (efficacious grace), which allows only God the power to bestow grace on human beings. Related to the Jesuits' use of the term 'grâce suffisante' is the expression 'pouvoir prochain' (proximate power), which concerns human power to achieve grace.

In Letters 4-10 , Pascal displays his sharp satirical skills. Having been in a defensive mode, now he moves onto the offensive. His use of the interplay between the naïve persona, the knowing and reasonable Jansenist friend and the bumbling buffoon-like Jesuit is worthy of the most effective Molière scenes, a point not lost on some contemporary readers. Racine, for example, wrote of *Lettres provinciales*:

> Et vous semble-t-il que les *Lettres Provinciales* soient autre chose que des comédies? Dites-moi, Messieurs, qu'est-ce qui se passe dans les comédies? On y joue un valet fourbe, un bourgeois avare, un marquis extravagant, et tout ce qu'il y a dans le monde de plus digne de risée. J'avoue que le Provincial a mieux choisi ses personnages: il les a cherchés dans les couvents et dans la Sorbonne; il introduit sur la scène tantôt des jacobins, tantôt des docteurs, et toujours des jésuites. Combien de rôles leur fait-il jouer! Tantôt il amène un jésuite bonhomme, tantôt un jésuite méchant, et toujours un jésuite ridicule.
>
> *Oeuvres complètes*, (Paris, 1966) vol 2, p. 29

(And do you think that the *Provincial Letters* are anything other than theatrical comedies? Tell me, Messieurs, what takes place in comedies? We find a crooked valet, a greedy bourgeois, an extravagant marquis, and everything in the world worthy of laughter. I declare that the Provincial has chosen his charcaters even better: he has hunted them out in convents and in the Sorbonne; he introduces to the stage now Jacobins, now religious Doctors and always Jesuits. And how many roles he makes them play! Now he brings on a goodly Jesuit, now a wicked Jesuit, and always a ridiculous Jesuit.)

In the fourth letter, the skilful interplay between the different personalities is particularly effective. We as readers share in Montalte's status as an uninformed person, therefore learning about the issues in a seemingly natural way. The addition of the emotive, irascible, wordy Jesuit and the sensible, knowing, unwordy Jansenist gives the dialogue a keen edge, making us side with the calm Jansenist, which is clearly the intention of the letter. At the end of the letter, the disparity between the different characters is underlined by the fact that, after a discussion of doctrine in which the Jesuit priest is unable to find adequate answers, he leaves in haste, offering the excuse that he has to see other people:

– J'en parlerai, dit-il, à nos Pères. Ils y trouveront bien quelque réponse. Nous en avons ici de bien subtils.
Nous l'entendîmes bien; et quand je fus seul avec mon ami, je lui témoignai d'être étonné du renversement que cette doctrine apportait dans la morale. A quoi il me répondit qu'il était bien étonné de mon étonnement.

Lafuma edition, pp. 386-7

(– I will speak of this to our holy Fathers, he said. They will certainly find some reply. We are dealing with very difficult problems here. We understood what he was saying, and when I was alone with my friend I admitted to him that I was astonished at the turnabout in morality of this doctrine. To which he replied that he was astonished at my astonishment.)

The play on the word 'étonné' shows both Montalte's naïvety and the Jansenist's control of the situation. It was a technique which Voltaire would use equally successfully the following century in *Candide* when he contrasts the innocent eponymous hero with the knowing Martin: 'On jouait gros jeu. Candide était tout étonné que jamais les as ne lui vinssent; et Martin ne s'en étonnait pas.' (They were gambling. Candide was astonished that the aces never fell to him, and Martin was not astonished) (Chapter XXII).

By using an interview technique (rather like modern journalism), Pascal manages to make the Jesuits condemn themselves out of their own mouths. The selective choice of quotation from Jesuit writers, which was noted and criticized by the Jesuits in their counter-polemic, forms an important part of this satire. In letter 5, the Jesuit lists various names of writers worth reading. All the names (many of which are concocted by Pascal) would be foreign-sounding to the French reader, inevitably making them appear less accessible. Moreover, the conversation which ensues succeeds in making the Jesuits appear narrow-minded, because of their apparent decision to allow only their own kind or at least those who refer to them in glowing terms to represent the Church. The Jansenists believed strongly that the Jesuits preferred their own recent writers to the ancient Church Fathers:

> – O mon Père! lui dis-je tout effrayé, tous ces gens-là étaient-ils chrétiens?
> – Comment, chrétiens! me répondit-il. Ne vous disais-je pas que ce sont les seuls par lesquels nous gouvernons aujourd'hui la chrétienté?
> Cela me fit pitié, mais je ne lui en témoignai rien, et lui demandai seulement si tous ces auteurs-là étaient Jésuites.
> – Non, me dit-il; mais il n'importe; ils n'ont pas laissé de dire de bonnes choses. Ce n'est pas que la plupart ne les aient pas prises ou imitées des nôtres; mais nous ne nous piquons pas d'honneur; outre qu'ils citent nos Pères à toute heure, et avec éloge.
>
> Lafuma edition, p. 391

(– Oh Father! I cried out, in a state of terror, were all these people
Christians? – What do you mean Christians! he replied. Didn't I tell
you that they are the only ones through whom we govern Christen-
dom today? That saddened me, but I did not let him know any of
this, and I simply asked him if all these authors were Jesuits. – No,
he said, but that doesn't matter; they still said many a good thing.
It is true that most of them took or copied from our authors; but we
do not make a point of honour out of it, especially as at all moments
they quote our Fathers, and in laudatory terms too.)

Letter 8 signals the first shift of tone. The naïve Montalte is for the
first time standing up for his own opinions. The seriousness of his
tone is off-set by the buffoon-like laughter of the Jesuit:

– Je crois que vous raillez, dit le Père; cela n'est pas bien. Car si vous
parliez ainsi en des lieux où vous ne fussiez pas connu, il pourrait se
trouver des gens qui prendraient mal vos discours, et qui vous
reprocheraient de tourner les choses de la religion en raillerie.
– Je me défendrais facilement de ce reproche, mon Père. Car je
crois que, si on prend la peine d'examiner le véritable sens de mes
paroles, on n'en trouvera aucune qui ne marque parfaitement le
contraire; et peut-être s'offrira-t-il un jour, dans nos entretiens,
l'occasion de le faire amplement paraître.
– Ho! ho! dit le Père, vous ne riez plus.

Lafuma edition, p. 407

(– I think you are joking, said the Father, and that is not good. For
if you spoke like this in places where you were not known, some
people might take your words in the wrong way and might reproach you for turning things of religion into a joke. – I would easily
defend myself from such a reproach, my Father. For I think that if
they take the trouble to examine the true meaning of my words,
they will not find a single word which does not indicate exactly the
opposite; and perhaps the opportunity will present itself in our
conversations one of these days to show this more fully. – Ha! Ha!
said the Father, you are not laughing now.)

Letters 11-18

From this point, we find the abandonment of the Montalte persona. Here the polemicist defends himself against the many accusations of misrepresentation made by the counter-polemicists. Their criticisms were focused mainly on his use of various Jesuit sources, as they claimed that he mistranslated various passages, made selective additions and omissions, changed the emphasis in places and (most serious of all) made serious religious topics seem comical. All these letters are now much more solemn in tone. Letters 11-16 are addressed 'aux Révérends Pères Jésuites', while the final two letters are directed specifically at one of the counter-polemicists, Père Annat, who was a leading Jesuit and, most significantly, the King's confessor.

On both sides of the polemic, claims of orthodoxy are made, especially with regard to the Church fathers. Whereas the Jesuit side attempted to reclaim St Augustine as their own guide, especially after the accusation that they only referred to modern pro-Jesuit thinkers, Pascal (stung by accusations that he was countering the teaching of St Thomas Aquinas) quotes Thomas approvingly in the later letters. As has been shown in the previous chapters, the need to refer to the old teachings in order to add weight to arguments is a constant factor in the seventeenth century. In an age so governed by tensions, it was seen to be safer to look back at a former age for an authority which could not argue back.

This debate between the Jesuits and Jansenists was to continue throughout the century. Those at Port-Royal and Port-Royal-des-Champs were continually persecuted and made to sign various *formulaires* (statements) condemning Jansenius, Arnauld and others. It culminated in Louis XIV disbanding and destroying the buildings of Port-Royal-des-Champs in 1709. Pockets of Jansenist sympathizers survived, but they were never again to be such a potent force.

As we saw with Molière, Pascal, transforming the debates of his time into theatre, managed to make what could have been an obscure and dull theological debate into an entertaining yet hard-hitting satire. In addition to the increasing tensions within the Church, a widely perceived threat from outside the Church was the growing circle of sceptics and unbelievers. In his *Pensées*, unfinished at the time of his early death in 1662, Pascal was to move from the internal wrangles of Jesuits and Jansenists, where at least the existence of God was accepted by both sides, to the more fundamental problem of trying to persuade doubters of the necessity to believe in the Christian God.

2. *Pensées*

There were many religious apologists in the first half of the seventeenth century, all seeking to save souls through different methods. In an age where prominent independent thinkers were either burnt at the stake (such as the free-thinker Vanini) or imprisoned (such as the poet Théophile de Viau), it is not surprising that few anti-Christian tracts survive from the early period of the seventeenth century. However, those works which were written expressly to refute atheism and unbelief show the level of suspicion in which these circles were held by the Church. Amongst various wild estimates of the number of atheists harboured in France, Marin Mersenne's assessment that there were fifty thousand in Paris alone must be the most over-inflated. Two prominent books attacking the *libertins* (free-thinkers) of the time are Mersenne's own *Impiété des déistes, athées et libertins de ce temps* (1624) and Garasse's *Doctrine curieuse des beaux esprits* (1623). As Mersenne's title implies, deists, atheists and *libertins* are equally impious. Deists expressed belief in a single God independent of Christianity, but, unlike in the eighteenth century where deism became a rationalist system of philosophy, the term was used more generally in the seventeenth century to describe the unbeliever. Mersenne devotes much of the book to a refutation of the anonymously published *Quatrains du déiste*, which explicitly rejects all notions of Heaven and Hell and the doctrine of original sin. The methods of persuasion employed by both Mersenne and

Garasse are direct. First, unbelievers are left in no doubt as to the awful fate which will await them if they choose not to follow the path prescribed by the Church. Second, from the outset the sceptic is depicted in the most unflattering terms possible. Mersenne, for example, speaking of deists, refers to 'la malice et infidélité de leurs esprits' (the malice and faithlessness of their minds), adding that 'ce me sont des objets insupportables aussi bien que les misères qui les environnent de toutes parts' (they are unbearable in my mind as are the wretched things which surround them on all sides). Garasse is even more uncompromising: 'J'appelle Libertins, nos ivrognets, moucherons de tavernes, esprits insensibles à la piété, qui n'ont autre Dieu que leur ventre' (I call free-thinkers our drunkards, bar-flies, minds insensible to piety, who have no God other than their stomachs). It is unlikely that unbelievers reading these words would have had the patience or perseverance to continue filling their stomachs with such invective. The rhetoric of treatises like these fails precisely because they do not take into account the opposing points of view of the very people they are attempting to persuade.

Pascal, on the other hand, takes a very different course of persuasion in his *Pensées*. Rather than steamrollering all opposition, he attempts to understand the psychology of his sceptical reader. As the century progressed, more outspoken sceptics, such as the rationalist Gabriel Naudé (1600-1653) and François de la Mothe le Vayer (1588-1672), emerged. Moreover, from the mathematical and scientific circles which Pascal frequented as a child and young man, he came into close contact with many erudite thinkers who were eager to question different schools of thought. As a result, he read avidly the writings of Michel de Montaigne (1533-1592), whose *Essais* were greatly to influence sceptics in the seventeenth century. He also became friendly with two active participants in the worldly circles of Paris, the chevalier de Méré (1604-1684) and Damien Mitton (1618-1690). Méré, although not mentioned by name in the *Pensées*, was well known as a gambler and is thought to have influenced Pascal in his work on the theory of probability.

Mitton's name, on the other hand, appears three times, each time as a putative sceptical interlocutor. Significantly, both were theorists of *honnêteté*, which I shall discuss in the next chapter. Pascal absorbs these different worldly influences in the *Pensées*, thereby giving the sense of a breadth of opinion which was missing in earlier apologetic texts. Similarly, in the *Entretien avec M. de Sacy*, which is the record of conversations which Pascal had with his spiritual director, Louis-Isaac Le Maître de Sacy (1613-1684), Pascal asserts the value of having read worldly writers such as Montaigne and the Stoic Epictetus, who were considered by religious authorities to be dangerous influences. Precisely because, as he sees it, these two writers were 'les deux plus grands défenseurs des deux plus célèbres sectes du monde' (the two greatest defenders of the most famous sects in the world), it is important to understand both their positive and negative points:

> Je trouve dans Epictète un art incomparable pour troubler le repos de ceux qui le cherchent dans les choses extérieures […]. Montaigne est incomparable pour confondre l'orgueil de ceux qui, hors la foi, se piquent d'une véritable justice; pour désabuser ceux qui s'attachent à leurs opinions, et qui croient trouver dans les sciences des vérités inébranlables; […]
> Mais si Epictète combat la paresse, il mène à l'orgueil, de sorte qu'il peut être très nuisible à ceux qui ne sont pas persuadés de la corruption de la plus parfaite justice qui n'est pas de la foi. Et Montaigne est absolument pernicieux à ceux qui ont quelque pente à l'impiété et aux vices.
>
> Lafuma edition, p. 297

(I find in Epictetus an art which is incomparable for disrupting the peace of those who seek it in external things. Montaigne is incomparable for confounding the pride of those who, outside faith, pride themselves on attaining true justice, for disabusing those who attach too much weight to their own opinions and who think they can find unshakable truths in science. But if Epictetus combats laziness, he can lead to pride, in a way that can be harmful to those who are not persuaded by the corruption of even the most perfect justice which is not related to faith. And Montaigne is absolutely pernicious for those who lean towards impiety and vice.)

Moreover, the dominant imagery used by Pascal in the *Pensées* would appeal particularly to the worldly circles for which he is most likely to have been writing. Perhaps the most famous passage from the *Pensées* is that known as the Wager, where he uses both mathematical arguments and gambling imagery to persuade his reader of the necessity to wager for the existence of God. Far from being a mathematical attempt to prove the existence of God, as some critics have maintained, the Wager engages the sceptical reader's attention first and foremost. Having argued that we as humans are obliged to play the game, because we are part of the game of life whether we like it or not ('vous êtes embarqués', you are engaged), Pascal weighs up the losses and gains (in other words, the odds) of betting that God does or does not exist. Ultimately, the only proof that we find is that mathematical proofs do not work in matters of religion. He has used deliberately worldly imagery in order first to seduce and then to force the unbeliever into contemplating religious belief.

Elsewhere in the *Pensées*, wide-ranging images reflect the leisure pursuits of Pascal's privileged readers. In the long fragment on *divertissement* (136), for example, gambling, hunting, wars, dancing, even billiards are evoked. Yet, while these images inevitably appeal to the designated reader, they are used precisely to demonstrate the futility of such activities in the pursuit of true happiness. Along with recognition of shared pleasurable pursuits should come a deeper recognition of the need to search elsewhere for spiritual peace. Although Pascal himself could be termed a political conservative, as he advocated (albeit from a pragmatic point of view) the acceptance of the monarchical and aristocratic status quo, he was not afraid to allude to the very highest authorities as examples of human wretchedness. Continuing the theme of *divertissement*, for example, he remarks that 'un roi sans divertissement est un homme plein de misères' (137) (a King with no diversions is a man full of wretched things).

As we saw from the earlier quotation from *Ecrits sur la grâce*, Pascal's adherence to Augustinian thought is firmly based in the idea of the two states or natures of man. According to him, the only way that we can explain human restlessness and contradictoriness is through the doctrine of the Fall, when Adam ate the apple in the Garden of Eden. Before the Fall, we were innocent. After the Fall, we became corrupt. Inevitably, as he sees it, our very beings are shaped by tensions, because we have a sense of our original perfection and are all too aware of our present imperfection.

In the *Pensées*, one of the most forceful expositions of the doctrine of the Fall, fragment 131, is a masterly display of the way in which Pascal coaxes his sceptical reader into paying attention to his arguments. Unlike Garasse or Mersenne, he does not begin by condemning his potential reader. Instead, he uses flattery. In the seventeenth century, the term most commonly applied to sceptics was *pyrrhoniens*, named originally after the Greek sceptic philosopher Pyrrho of Elis (c. 300 B.C.) but used particularly by Pascal to describe followers of Montaigne. Perhaps the most characteristic opinion of the sceptics was their espousal of Montaigne's statement, 'Que sais-je?' (What do I know?), where all knowledge is deemed to be uncertain. Pascal begins fragment 131 by praising them: 'Les principales forces des pyrrhoniens, je laisse les moindres, sont que nous n'avons aucune certitude de la vérité de ces principes [...]' (The main strengths of the sceptics, and I will not mention the lesser ones, are that we have no certainty of the truth of these principles). The 'principes' about which sceptics believed there to be no certainty are known as first principles, usually accepted by all, such as time, space, numbers. In this passage, the sceptics are praised for throwing into question those aspects about which we might be complacent (such as distinguishing between whether we are awake or in fact dreaming about being awake). The comment, 'je laisse les moindres', is a standard rhetorical ploy known as paralipsis, where a writer or speaker emphasizes a point by seeming to pass over it. Despite claiming not to mention the lesser strengths of the sceptics, he does precisely that a little later, thereby flattering their self-esteem: 'Voilà les principales forces de part et d'autre, je laisse les moindres comme les discours qu'ont faits les pyrrhoniens contre les impressions de la coutume, de l'éducation, des moeurs des pays, et les autres choses semblables [...]' (those are generally the main strengths; I will not mention the lesser ones, such as the speeches made by sceptics against the impressions caused by custom, education, each country's mores, and other similar things).

Having gained at least the good will of the sceptical reader, Pascal then moves to the principal opponents of the sceptics, the rationalists (or 'dogmatistes', as he calls them). While being less indulgent towards them, nonetheless, he praises them for one aspect of their thought: 'Je m'arrête à l'unique fort des dogmatistes qui est qu'en parlant de bonne foi et sincèrement on ne peut douter des principes naturels' (I will stop at the one strength of the dogmatists which is that, speaking in all good faith and sincerely, we cannot doubt natural principles). Significantly, he praises the dogmatists for exactly the opposite reason that he first praised the sceptics: the dogmatists' belief in first principles. By deliberately applauding both sides' contrasting viewpoints, he sets each sect in direct confrontation with each other. Pascal as the speaker removes himself from the argument by simply posing the different viewpoints of pyrrhonists and dogmatists, leading eventually to an acknowledgement of the open conflict between both sides:

> Voilà la guerre ouverte entre les hommes, où il faut que chacun prenne parti, et se range nécessairement ou au dogmatisme ou au pyrrhonisme. Car qui pensera demeurer neutre sera pyrrhonien par excellence. Cette neutralité est l'essence de la cabale. Qui n'est pas contre eux est excellemment pour eux: en quoi paraît leur avantage.

> (From there we find open warfare between men, where each person must take a stance and go to the side of either the sceptics or the

dogmatists. For whoever will think of remaining neutral will be the sceptic par excellence. This neutrality forms the essence of their conspiracy. Whoever is not against them is greatly for them: in which appears their advantage.)

Rather as the unbeliever is forced to wager for or against the existence of God in the Wager, here one has to choose between dogmatism and scepticism. By claiming not to be on either side, one is automatically on the sceptics' side, because of the centrality of uncertainty ('Que sais-je?') to their doctrine. In this way, again the sceptical reader has been flattered into maintaining the upper hand in the argument. Yet, the verb 'paraître' signals that this advantage is perhaps only an illusion.

By posing several questions about the role which doubt plays in the sceptics' beliefs, using *reductio ad absurdum* (a method of proving the falsity of a premiss by demonstrating that the logical consequence is absurd), Pascal shows their arguments to be self-defeating:

> Que fera l'homme en cet état? doutera-t-il de tout, doutera-t-il s'il veille, si on le pince, si on le brûle, doutera-t-il s'il doute, doutera-t-il s'il est? On n'en peut venir là, et je mets en fait qu'il n'y a jamais eu de pyrrhonien effectif parfait.

> (What will man do in this state? will he doubt everything, will he doubt if he is awake, if he has been pinched or burnt, will he doubt if he is doubting, will he doubt if he exists? It is impossible to go that far, and I put it that there has never been an effectively perfect sceptic.)

At this stage in the argument, Pascal again launches into a series of questions, but this time, having used the conflict between pyrrhonists and dogmatists as a starting point, he underlines the contradictory nature of all humans by listing widely diverging states of man. The coupling of antitheses (such as 'gloire' and 'rebut') only serves to unsettle the reader:

Quelle chimère est-ce donc que l'homme? quelle nouveauté, quel monstre, quel chaos, quel sujet de contradictions, quel prodige? Juge de toutes choses, imbécile ver de terre, dépositaire du vrai, cloaque d'incertitude et d'erreur, gloire et rebut de l'univers.

(What dream is man then? what novelty, monster, chaos, contradictory subject, prodigy? Judge over all things, imbecile worm of the earth, depository of truth, sewer of uncertainty and error, glory and scrapheap of the universe.)

He then poses the leading question, 'Qui démêlera cet embrouillement?' (Who will unravel this chaos?), before moving to a series of imperatives. The time for questioning is over. The sceptical reader has been coaxed and questioned. Unlike in earlier religious apologies, where an immediate attack on the unbeliever would in all likelihood have alienated the sceptical reader, it is only at this late stage of the argument that Pascal commences his assault. General questions give way to direct use of 'vous':

Connaissez donc, superbe, quel paradoxe vous êtes à vous-même. Humiliez-vous, raison impuissante! Taisez-vous, nature imbécile, apprenez que l'homme passe infiniment l'homme et entendez de votre maître votre condition véritable que vous ignorez.

(Know then, o proud person, what a paradox you are to yourself. Humble yourself, powerless reason! Be quiet, imbecile nature, learn that man infinitely surpasses man and learn from your master your real condition of which you are ignorant.)

Only at this stage, writing in a separate paragraph so as to emphasize its significance, does he give his solution: 'Ecoutez Dieu' (Listen to God). The remainder of the fragment is devoted to his explanation of the contradictions within human nature: the doctrine of the Fall. Rather than avoiding tensions, he embraces them so as to explain our paradoxical selves:

Car enfin si l'homme n'avait jamais été corrompu il jouirait dans son innocence et de la vérité et de la félicité avec assurance. Et si l'homme n'avait jamais été que corrompu il n'aurait aucune idée ni de la vérité, ni de la béatitude. Mais malheureux que nous sommes et plus que s'il n'y avait point de grandeur dans notre condition, nous avons une idée du bonheur et nous ne pouvons y arriver. Nous sentons une idée de la vérité et ne possédons que le mensonge. Incapables d'ignorer absolument et de savoir certainement, tant il est manifeste que nous avons été dans un degré de perfection dont nous sommes malheureusement déchus.

(For in the end if man had never been corrupt, he would with assurance and in his innocence enjoy truth and happiness. And if man had always been corrupt, he would have no idea of either truth or eternal happiness. But unhappy as we are (and we would be less so if our condition had never had any greatness in it), we have an idea of happiness and yet we cannot attain it. We sense an idea of truth and yet we possess only falsehood. Incapable of not knowing completely and of knowing certainly, it is so manifest that we were once in a state of perfection from which we have unhappily fallen.)

In an age where, either from a rationalist perspective or for an apologetic purpose, comprehensive terms such as 'vérité' or 'justice' are sometimes simplified, Pascal accentuates their complexity. From a rationalist standpoint, Descartes, for example, stresses in his *Discours de la méthode* that truth can be attained through reason, claiming that 'la puissance de bien juger et distinguer le vrai d'avec le faux, qui est proprement ce qu'on nomme le bon sens ou la raison, est naturellement égale dans tous les hommes' (the power of judging well and distinguishing true from false, which we properly call common sense or reason, is naturally equal in all men). Pascal, on the other hand, makes the claim that distinguishing between truth and falsity is by no means so easy: 'La justice et la vérité sont deux pointes si subtiles que nos instruments sont trop mousses pour y toucher exactement. S'ils y arrivent ils en écachent la pointe et appuient tout autour plus sur le faux que sur le vrai.' (Justice and truth are two such subtle points that our instruments are too blunt to touch them precisely. If they do meet they blunt the point and press more on the false than the true) (Lafuma 44).

Similarly, where another apologist such as Jean de Silhon in his *Les Deux vérités* (1626) rigidly delineates truths at the very beginning of his book as being 'l'une de Dieu et de sa providence, l'autre de l'immortalité de l'âme' (one is of God and his providence, the other of the immortality of the soul), Pascal again allows for the complexity of truth and the many different truths that exist.

I shall return to a discussion of Pascal in Chapter 6 (on genre), where his use of the fragment can be seen as crucial to his understanding of the complexity of human nature and to his persuasive project.

Both the *Lettres provinciales* and the *Pensées* were read avidly in many circles in Paris, most notably in the literary salons. It was in these groups that two recurring terms in the seventeenth century, *préciosité* and *honnêteté*, flourished and took on lives and indeed tensions of their own.

Selected Reading

General:

A.J. Krailsheimer, *Pascal* (Oxford, 1980). Part of the *Past Masters* series, and a good introduction to Pascal.

B. Pascal, *Oeuvres complètes*, ed. L. Lafuma (Paris 1963). The most accessible edition of Pascal's works.

H. Phillips, *Church and Culture in Seventeenth-Century France* (Cambridge, 1997). A useful overview of many disputes within the Church, though more concerned with historical and cultural phenomena than with the literature of the period.

Lettres provinciales:

R. Parish, *Pascal's Lettres provinciales: a study in polemic* (Oxford, 1989). Especially interesting on the Jesuit counter-polemic, but also excellent as a detailed study of the fields of debate.

W. Rex, *Pascal's Provincial Letters: an introduction* (London, 1977). Useful historical and theological background.

Pensées:

N. Hammond, *Playing with Truth: language and the human condition in Pascal's*

Pensées (Oxford, 1994). Analysis of the persuasive strategies and use of language in the *Pensées*.

J. Mesnard, *Les Pensées de Pascal* (Paris, 1976). In French. Probably the best general study in French on the *Pensées*.

D. Wetsel, *Pascal and Disbelief: catechesis and conversion in the Pensées* (Washington, 1994). Most interesting on the kinds of reader for whom Pascal was writing.

Honnêteté and *Préciosité*

As I mentioned in the last chapter, religious controversies were eagerly followed in literary and *mondain* (fashionable) circles. It was in these groups that codes of living, behaving and indeed speaking were discussed. The two terms which most often have been used to describe many of these codes, *honnêteté* and *préciosité*, can justifiably be seen as crucial to our understanding of society from that time.

On a superficial level, both terms would seem to be uncomplicated. *Honnêteté* is generally associated with fundamental decency, civilized behaviour and moderation. *Préciosité*, on the other hand, has come to be linked particularly with society women of the day, implying above all affectation and verbosity. I shall discuss in this chapter fundamental tensions within both concepts, especially with reference to problems of class, gender and religion.

One work which in its opening pages appears to incarnate both the ideals of *honnêteté* (with its appeal to the civilization of a former aristocratic age) and the *précieux* language of the salons is *La Princesse de Clèves* (1678), published anonymously but generally accepted to be by Mme de Lafayette. The very first sentence evokes a seventeenth-century perception of this civilized sixteenth-century world: 'La magnificence et la galanterie n'ont jamais paru en France avec tant d'éclat que dans les dernières années du règne de Henri second' (Never has France experienced such a display of magnificence and courtly manners as in the final years of Henri II's reign). The words 'magnificence' and 'galanterie' would appear to epitomize the perfection of court life. Yet, the status of the term 'galanterie' is thrown into question and indeed has a different sense only a few pages later, when we learn that:

> L'ambition et la galanterie étaient l'âme de cette cour, et occupaient également les hommes et les femmes. Il y avait tant d'intérêts et tant de cabales différentes, et les dames y avaient tant de part que l'amour était toujours mêlé aux affaires et les affaires à l'amour. Personne n'était tranquille, ni indifférent; on songeait à s'élever, à plaire, à servir ou à nuire; on ne connaissait ni l'ennui, ni l'oisiveté, et on était toujours occupé des plaisirs ou des intrigues.

> (Ambition and love affairs were the life-blood of this court, involving men and women equally. There were countless personal interests and different factions, and the women played such an integral role in these that love was always mingled with political affairs and vice versa. Nobody was calm or indifferent; everyone was concerned with advancement, pleasing others, helping or harming; boredom and idleness were unknown and everyone was involved in pleasures or intrigue.)

The restlessness which characterizes court life in *La Princesse de Clèves* inevitably undermines any stability and order which may be associated with such concepts as 'galanterie'. *Honnêteté* is similarly complex.

1. *Honnêteté*

The definition of *honnêteté* as 'Bienséance, Civilité' (Propriety, Civility) which is offered by the 1694 *Dictionnaire de l'Académie française* could easily be applied to the surface order and politeness of the court in *La Princesse de Clèves*. However, it does not account for the complexity of the term. Furetière's *Dictionnaire universel* (1690) uncovers, albeit unwittingly, a fundamental disparity between the *honnêteté* of women and that of men, which in turn could be applied on the one hand to the expectations imposed upon the princess and on the other to the actions of her suitor, the duc de Nemours. While an *honnête* woman should be chaste and pure, no such restraint is imposed on an *honnête* man, who is expected to act in a civilized manner. Significantly, the woman is further restricted in the following definition by a sequence of inflexible nouns, whereas the man is defined by infinitely more malleable adjectives:

> L'honnêteté des femmes, c'est la chasteté, la modestie, la pudeur, la retenue.
> L'honnêteté des hommes, est une manière d'agir juste, sincère, courtoise, obligeante, civile.

> (The *honnêteté* of women is: chastity, modesty, discretion and restraint. The *honnêteté* of men is: a manner of acting in a just way, sincere, courtly, obliging and civil.)

I shall consider this discrepancy later in this chapter.

In Chapter 1, I warned against the too easy classification of the seventeenth century into Baroque and Classicisme. Similarly, we should be wary of placing *honnêteté* into simplistic categories. One of the twentieth century's foremost scholars of seventeenth-century French literature, Jean Mesnard, falls precisely into this trap when discussing *honnêteté*. He offers a detailed and learned reading of many texts associated with *honnêteté*, but chooses to see the term as both tension-free and falling into clearly marked areas of the century:

> Toute tension est ainsi exclue; le stoïcisme est dépassé. Ce n'est pas seulement un idéal d'humanité qui se définit, mais toute une esthétique, fondée sur une culture dont les valeurs s'opposent à celles de l'âge baroque et laissent présager le classicisme.
> *La Culture du XVIIe siècle*, (Paris, 1992) p. 147

> (All tension is therefore excluded; stoicism is surpassed. It is not only an ideal of humanity which is defined here, but a whole aesthetic code, based on a culture whose values are opposed to those values of the baroque age which allow a foretaste of classicism.)

The multi-dimensional nature both of the century and of *honnêteté* itself are inevitably over-simplified by such categorization.

Honnêteté and Class Distinctions

To a large extent, ideas of *honnêteté* were formed as much by literary sources from classical and more recent times as by models of behaviour of contemporary examples. In other words, reality and literary representations of reality were often fused together.

The work which was perhaps most influential in the formation of French seventeenth-century definitions of *honnêteté* emanated from Italy. Baldesar Castiglione's *Il Cortegiano* (1528), first translated into French in 1537, was closely related to the concept of *courtoisie*, a term which became unfashionable in seventeenth-century France but which was replaced by words like *politesse* and *honnêteté*. Castiglione's concerns were founded upon codes of politeness exclusively in courtly society, and such a bias is evident in a work both influenced by Castiglione and in its turn widely read in seventeenth-century France, Nicolas Faret's *L'Honnête homme ou l'Art de plaire à la cour* (1630). As the sub-title implies, Faret was principally interested in life surrounding the Court. Moreover, at the beginning of the book, he explicitly equates *honnêteté* with noble birth: 'je dirai premièrement qu'il me semble très nécessaire que celui qui veut entrer dans ce grand commerce du monde soit né Gentilhomme, et d'une maison qui ait quelque bonne marque' (I will say firstly that it seems very necessary to me that whoever wants to enter into this great worldly circle should be born a gentleman and from a house with a noble quality). However, rather than being a nobleman's hand-book for other noblemen, Faret's work is more complex in that it is written by a bourgeois for, amongst others, a bourgeois audience. For the first time, those outside the Court were being afforded glimpses of life within the Court. In other words, Faret's ideas of *honnêteté* can be perceived as representations of a world to which many readers could not belong. Two related terms which were used in France to describe *honnêtes gens* are also underpinned by questions of class: 'homme de qualité' is less directly associated with nobility, but 'homme de condition' is explicitly class-based.

It is perhaps not surprising to learn that Faret, who was so keen
to prescribe different kinds of noble and civilized behaviour to the
general public, was also a close friend of early members of the
Académie and in particular prominent promoters of the French
language, such as Guez de Balzac and Vaugelas.

If we consider an aristocrat's views on *honnêteté*, the perspective
is very different. The chevalier de Méré (1607-1684), whom I
mentioned in Chapter 5 as one of Pascal's worldly friends, wrote a
number of *discours* on matters such as conversation, wit and charm.
His *De la vraie honnêteté* (*Discours I, Oeuvres posthumes*), first published
after his death, makes the point that *honnêteté* should not be confined
to the Court: 'Je voudrais que pour se rendre l'honnêteté naturelle,
on ne l'aimât pas moins dans le fond d'un désert, qu'au milieu de
la Cour' (My wish would be that, in order for *honnêteté* to be made
a natural part of oneself, it should be loved no less in the depths of
a desert than in the middle of the Court). Whereas Faret sees the
honnête homme as part of an exclusive club, Méré claims that *honnêteté*
can be attained in different situations. Yet the problem is more
complex, crucially because Méré is writing from the perspective of
one who is already a member of the nobility. The examples which
he uses are concerned mainly with aristocratic pleasures, such as
dancing and hunting. Moreover, by stressing that *honnêteté* cannot
be taught, that it is innate, he is subscribing to an elitism which is
no less pronounced than that of Faret:

> Ce n'est donc pas un métier, que d'être honnête-homme; et si
> quelqu'un me demandait en quoi consiste l'honnêteté, je dirais que
> ce n'est autre chose que d'exceller en tout ce qui regarde les
> agréments et les bienséances de la vie.
>
> (Being an *honnête-homme* is not a job; if someone asked me what
> *honnêteté* consists of, I would say that it is nothing other than the
> ability to excel in everything to do with the pleasant manners and
> conventions of life.)

Pascal appears to offer a more general (and less exclusive) perception of *honnêteté*, but, like Méré, sees it as an inner quality: 'Il faut qu'on n'en puisse dire ni il est mathématicien, ni prédicateur, ni éloquent, mais il est honnête homme. Cette qualité universelle me plaît seule' (We must not say that he is a mathematician, or a preacher, or eloquent, but that he is an *honnête homme*. This universal quality alone is what I like) (*Pensées*, Lafuma 647). Elsewhere, he reiterates this point, emphasizing that it cannot be taught:

> On n'apprend point aux hommes à être honnêtes hommes, et on leur apprend tout le reste. Et ils ne se piquent jamais tant de savoir rien du reste comme d'être honnêtes hommes. Ils ne se piquent de savoir que la seule chose qu'ils n'apprennent point.
>
> *Pensées*, Lafuma 778

> (Men are never taught how to be *honnêtes hommes* but are taught everything else. And yet they never show as much interest in learning about everything else as they do about how to be *honnêtes hommes*. They are concerned only with knowing about the only thing which they cannot learn.)

The use of the verb 'se piquer de' (meaning either to become angry about or to feel strongly about or to be concerned with) indicates an interesting pattern, for it recurs especially frequently in writings of the time which treat the subject of *honnêteté*. One possible explanation for this repetition is that it was a verb widely used in salon conversations about *honnêteté*, and that it had become a commonplace. La Rochefoucauld, for example, who writes at length about *honnêteté*, asserts that 'le vrai honnête homme est celui qui ne se pique de rien' (the true *honnête homme* is the person who does not become angry about anything, *Maximes*, 203). For La Rochefoucauld, as for many other theoreticians of *honnêteté*, the true *honnête homme* maintains a '*juste milieu*' (appropriate middle ground) in all matters. However, this does not exclude a performative aspect to his functions. One must be held up to the view of others. As La Rochefoucauld sees it, 'c'est être véritablement honnête homme que de vouloir être toujours exposé à la vue des honnêtes gens' (to

be a genuine *honnête homme* one must be willing always to be held up
before the eyes of other *honnêtes* people) (*Maximes*, 206). Moreover,
although he may be widely read, he must affect a 'docte ignorance',
not appearing too learned. Even Descartes, founder of modern
rationalist philosophy, subscribes to this view. As he puts it at the
beginning of his *Recherche de la vérité par la lumière naturelle*, 'un
honnête homme n'est pas obligé d'avoir vu tous les livres' (an
honnête homme is not obliged to have seen all books).

Some proponents of *honnêteté* explicitly equate the measured
behaviour of the *honnête homme* with reason. Indeed, it was against
the reliance of thinkers like Descartes on human rational powers
that Pascal based many arguments in the *Pensées*. Another named
target in the *Pensées*, as I mentioned in the previous chapter, was the
free-thinker Damien Mitton, who himself wrote on *honnêteté*. In
addition to using the verb 'se piquer de', Mitton praises the *honnête
homme*'s use of reason:

> l'honnête homme fait grand cas de l'esprit, mais il fait encore plus
> de cas de la raison [...]. Il veut tout savoir et ne se pique de rien
> savoir; il prend garde à tout; il n'estime les choses que selon leur
> véritable valeur.
>
> *Description de l'honnête homme*

> (the *honnête homme* sees the importance of the spirit but even more of
> reason. He wishes to know everything but is not concerned at
> knowing nothing; he is aware of everything, and he values things
> only according to their true worth.)

One of Pascal's principal themes, especially in relation to his
sceptical interlocutor, is that of *amour-propre*, self-interest or self-
love, which he sees as dangerous because it is directly opposed to
the love of God. Mitton, in his *Pensées sur l'honnêteté*, links *honnêteté*
directly to *amour-propre*: 'C'est ce ménagement de bonheur pour
nous et pour les autres que l'on doit appeler l'honnêteté, qui n'est,
à le bien prendre, que l'amour propre bien réglé' (It is this handling
of happiness for ourselves and for others that should be termed

honnêteté, which in effect is nothing other than properly controlled self-interest). In one of the fragments where Pascal appeals to Mitton by name, it is precisely this concept of self-interest which he criticizes. Even if *amour-propre* is 'bien réglé', it is only a way of covering up man's essential self-centredness:

> Le moi est haïssable. Vous Mitton le couvrez, vous ne l'ôtez point pour cela. Vous êtes donc toujours haïssable.
>
> *Pensées,* Lafuma 597

> (The self is detestable. Mitton, you cover it up, but you do not take it away. You therefore are detestable.)

Honnêteté and Religion

In the earlier decades of the seventeenth century, *honnêteté* was rarely equated with religious thought. The implication of Pascal's criticism of Mitton is that religious belief does not play any significant part within the life of the *honnête homme.* He even goes on to state that Mitton understands the effect but not the cause of man's corruption:

> Mitton voit bien que la nature est corrompue et que les hommes sont contraires à l'honnêteté, mais il ne sait pas pourquoi ils ne peuvent voler plus haut.
>
> *Pensées,* 642

> (Mitton sees perfectly well that human nature is corrupt and that men oppose *honnêteté,* but he does not know why they cannot fly any higher.)

However, with the greater spiritual rigour which became prevalent in the 1680s and the emergence of religious opposition to *honnêteté,* especially amongst Augustinian thinkers, proponents of *honnêteté* felt it necessary to make the concept coexistent with the respectability of religion. Towards the end of his *discours,* Méré pays lip-service to the partnership of *honnêteté* and religion:

Je prends garde aussi, que la dévotion et l'honnêteté vont presque les mêmes voies, et qu'elles s'aident l'une à l'autre. La dévotion rend l'honnêteté plus solide et plus digne de confiance; et l'honnêteté comble la dévotion de bon air et d'agrément.

Discours II

(I take note also that religious devotion and *honnêteté* take almost the same routes and that they are mutually helpful to each other. Devotion makes *honnêteté* more solid and worthy of confidence, and *honnêteté* makes devotion both attractive and pleasurable.)

However, the tensions are immediately apparent in Méré's terminology. There seems to be little conviction in the comment that religion only serves to make *honnêteté* 'solide' and 'digne de confiance'. Moreover, conversely, the effect of *honnêteté* upon religion appears to be little more than decorative, as displayed in the words 'de bon air' and 'agrément'.

Writing for the seventh edition of his *Caractères* (1692), La Bruyère manages to underline both the evolving nature of the *honnête homme* and the more pragmatic approach to religion by relating it to the related terms '*habile homme*' and '*homme de bien*':

L'honnête homme tient le milieu entre l'habile homme et l'homme de bien, quoique dans une distance inégale de ces deux extrêmes.

La distance qu'il y a de l'honnête homme à l'habile homme s'affaiblit de jour à autre, et est sur le point de disparaître.

L'habile homme est celui qui cache ses passions, qui entend ses intérêts, qui y sacrifie beaucoup de choses, qui a su acquérir du bien, ou en conserver.

L'honnête homme est celui qui ne vole pas sur les grands chemins, et qui ne tue personne, dont les vices enfin ne sont pas scandaleux.

On connaît assez qu'un homme de bien est honnête homme; mais il est plaisant d'imaginer que tout honnête homme n'est pas homme de bien.

L'homme de bien est celui qui n'est ni un saint ni un dévot, et qui s'est borné à n'avoir que de la vertu.

Des jugements, XII, 55

(The *honnête homme* holds the middle ground between the cultivated man and the goodly man, although with an unequal distance from the two extremes. The distance between the *honnête homme* and the cultivated man becomes smaller by the day and is about to disappear. The cultivated man hides his passions, understands his own interests, sacrificing many things to them, having known how to acquire or keep goodly things. The *honnête homme* does not embark on the great roads of fame, does not kill anybody and his vices are not in the end scandalous. It is quite well known that a goodly man is an *honnête homme*; but it is amusing to imagine that not every *honnête homme* is a goodly man. The goodly man is neither a saint nor a devout person but someone who has restricted himself only to being virtuous.)

Honnêtes hommes and *Honnêtes femmes*

The comments about *honnêtes hommes* in texts are wide-ranging, but, as we saw in the Furetière dictionary definition, there exists a fundamental disparity between the perception of the *honnête homme* and the *honnête femme*. Many contradictions seem to exist, as a number of texts assert a certain kind of equality between men and women.

Faret, for example, writes in *L'Honnête Homme* that 'la générosité des femmes est la même que celle des hommes' (the magnanimity of women is the same as that of men) (p. 97). Moreover, Jacques Du Bosc's *L'Honnête Femme* (1632), which appeared two years after Faret's text, seems in many ways startlingly modern in its advocacy of equality. In the *Epître aux dames* at the head of the book, Du Bosc goes so far as to express his wish that his work will inspire in women 'le courage de rentrer dans les droits et de reprendre les avantages que la nature leur donne' (the courage to discover their rights and reclaim the advantages that nature bestows on them). He even sees in the institution of marriage a form of tyranny imposed by men on women: 'On dirait à voir dans leur tyrannie, que le mariage n'a été institué que pour donner des geôliers aux femmes' (One might say in the tyranny of men that marriage was only insituted to impose jailers on women) (p. 86).

Yet, many comments which on the surface appear complimentary towards women contain hidden problems. Let us take a statement by Du Bosc: 'Si le courage est l'avantage des hommes, la pureté est celui des femmes' (if courage is the advantage of men, purity is the advantage of women) (p. 426). Even while praising the advantages of women, he cannot avoid imposing a sexual straitjacket on them by his use of the noun 'pureté', thus implying moral control: in order to be pure, a woman must refrain from sexual contact. By contrast, the noun 'courage' which is used to describe men indicates an active life free of sexual restraint.

Similarly, La Bruyère's comparison of a woman to an *honnête homme* appears at first to be wholly positive: 'Une belle femme qui a les qualités d'un honnête homme est ce qu'il y a au monde d'un commerce plus délicieux: l'on trouve en elle tout le mérite des sexes' (A beautiful woman who has an *honnête homme*'s qualities contains the most delicious assortment in the world: all the merit of both sexes can be found in her) (*Les Caractères*, 'Des femmes', III, 13). Yet the woman is encumbered by the qualifying adjective 'belle', immediately restricting her to a physical object. Even when she is shown to have the (non-physical) 'qualités' of an *honnête homme*, those attributes are debased by the erotic qualifier 'délicieux'.

The chevalier de Méré is another *honnête* writer who upholds the virtues of women. In one passage, he values the listening to women's conversation as essential to true *honnêteté*: 'le commerce des honnêtes-gens est à rechercher; mais les entretiens des Dames, dont les grâces font penser aux bienséances, sont encore plus nécessaires pour s'achever dans l'honnêteté' (the interaction of *honnêtes* people is to be sought after, but women's conversations, whose gracious appearance makes one think of propriety are even more necessary to become fully accomplished as an *honnête* person) (*Discours* I, p. 75). Although women are therefore perceived by

Méré to play an important role in the formation of any *honnête homme*, the word 'bienséances', with which he directly associates women, again indicates moral restraint.

Women who classed themselves and were viewed by others as *honnêtes* inevitably belonged to the aristocracy. Many of them were members of intellectual circles which became associated with the term *préciosité*. Although these groups were dominated by women, it is clear that self-styled *honnêtes hommes* like Méré attended their meetings and were influenced by their conversations. Indeed, in the *Recueil de choses diverses*, which is a fascinating collection of conversations (written down by a scribe) which took place at the Hôtel de Liancourt in Paris between 1670 and 1671, Méré is directly linked to the précieuses. The comment, 'Monsieur Lumbert estime que le chevalier Méré est un livre précieux' (M. Lumbert thinks that the chevalier Méré is himself a *précieux* book), is accompanied by a remark in the margin, explaining, 'Il était collet monté et de l'école des Précieuses' (he wore a high collar and belonged to the school of *Précieuses*) (p. 276).

The juxtaposition of *honnêteté* and *préciosité* can be found also in the correspondence of Mme de Sévigné. Having belonged to a number of *précieux* circles which discouraged women from concerning themselves with such mundane realities as marriage and pregnancy, Mme de Sévigné wrote to her daughter (who was pregnant) on 21 October 1671, that 'l'honnêteté et la préciosité d'un long veuvage m'avaient laissée dans une profonde ignorance' (a long time of widowhood within *honnête* and *précieux* circles has left me profoundly ignorant).

2. Préciosité

By the time that the Furetière dictionary was published in 1690, the definition of the term *précieuse* shows the way in which the term had been debased in the course of the century:

Précieuse: une epithète qu'on a donnée [...] à des filles de grand mérite et de grande vertu, qui savaient bien le monde et la langue: mais parce que d'autres ont affecté et outré leurs manières, cela a décrié le mot.

(an epithet formerly given to young women of great merit and great virtue, who were perfectly conversant with both speaking and the world; but because others have affected and exaggerated their behaviour, the word has been debased.)

Initially, as the dictionary shows, the *précieuses* were particularly associated with 'le monde' and 'la langue'. These two categories best encapsulate the major salons with which the *précieuses* were associated.

The salon of Mme de Rambouillet, which was held at the Hôtel de Rambouillet in *la chambre bleue* (her bedroom), can best be termed *mondain* (fashionable), as it was less concerned with literary matters than political and social issues of the day. It was also more closely connected to the Court, as a number of eminent Court personalities, such as the duchesse de Longueville and her brother the prince de Condé, frequented Mme de Rambouillet's salon. These two figures, along with others who attended the salon, were instrumental in the period of civil insurrection known as the Fronde (1648-53), the revolt against the policies of cardinal Mazarin which limited the fiscal powers of both the nobility and the royal government. The fact that women, including the duchesse de Longueville and the duchesse de Montpensier, were closely involved in these political stirrings gave women a more prominent status. I shall return to this issue in Chapter 7.

It was at the time of the Fronde, 1648, that Mme de Rambouillet's salon began to break up (due in part to a number of its participants fleeing Paris). But it was largely replaced by a salon which was primarily concerned with language and literary matters, that of Madeleine de Scudéry (1608-1701), the prolific writer of historical prose fiction. Two of her novels, *Artamène, ou le grand Cyrus* (1649-53) and particularly *Clélie* (1654-60), can be said to emanate directly from salon life, both in the use of language which came to be known as *précieux* and in the portraits of various personalities associated with the salon. I shall discuss the portrait as a genre in Chapter 6. Between 1653 and 1661, both the *précieuses* and Mlle de Scudéry's salon, known as *le samedi* (named, not surprisingly, after the day on which it met) enjoyed their heyday. Antoine Somaize's *Le Grand dictionnaire des précieuses* (1660, 1661) proves the popularity of *préciosité* at the time and contains portraits mostly of women but also of some men who were directly associated with the salons and with *préciosité*. However, already the *précieuses* had become the target of satirists.

Précieuses as Object of Satire

The excesses, especially linguistic, of the *précieuses* were ruthlessly satirized. As a result, the distortion became more famous than the original model.

Molière's *Précieuses ridicules* (1659) is perhaps the most celebrated example of such satire. In the play, characters mimic the favourite expressions of the salons. To take just one short extract:

Madelon: Il faudrait être l'antipode de la raison, pour ne pas confesser que Paris est le grand bureau des merveilles, le centre du bon goût, du bel esprit, et de la galanterie.
Mascarille: Pour moi, je tiens que hors de Paris il n'y a point de salut pour les honnêtes gens.

scene IX

(Madelon: One would have to be at the furthest point from reason not to admit that Paris is the great focus of marvels, the centre of good taste, witty minds and civility. Mascarille: In my opinion, there is no salvation for *honnêtes* people outside Paris.)

It is interesting to note that here also *honnêteté* is linked to *préciosité*. The *précieux* and *précieuses* were in many ways an extreme case of the cultivated *honnêtes gens*. Madelon's reference to 'raison', 'bon goût', 'bel esprit' and 'galanterie' is typical of the concerns of many *honnêtes gens*, as we have already seen in this chapter. However, it was the *précieuses*' precise and over-detailed attention to matters of style, taste and language that made them vulnerable to satire.

In response, Somaize, great champion of the *précieuses*, wrote a play in their defence, entitled *Les Véritables Précieuses* (1660), but by this stage the negative connotations had taken hold.

Précieuses as Positive Force

It is clear that, even though some of the laughter directed at the affectation of the *précieuses* was justified, much of the hostility to-wards them stemmed from the self-empowerment of women within the salons. Not only did the women assert their ability to think independently but also they challenged the conventions of the patriarchal society in which they lived by opposing the subser-vient role which women were forced to take in daily life, intellectual matters and marriage itself. Often they were depicted as viragos or prudes by their critics. It is not difficult to see in this opposition to them an inner agenda by men who resented the *précieuses*' intellec-tual freedom.

Although Molière mocked the verbal excesses of the *précieuses* in *Les Précieuses ridicules*, he was no less keen to satirize men's attitude towards the *précieuses*' independence. Arnolphe's attitude to women in *L'Ecole des femmes* perhaps typifies the position of the most viru-lent critics of the *précieuses*. While congratulating himself on keeping his prospective bride Agnès locked up, Arnolphe attempts to mimic the *précieux* language of the day by proclaiming his superiority over those creative women who meet in the salons:

> Héroïnes du temps, mesdames les savantes,
> Pousseuses de tendresse et de beaux sentiments,
> Je défie à la fois tous vos vers, vos romans,
> Vos lettres, billets doux, toute votre science,
> De valoir cette honnête et pudique ignorance.

> I, 3, 244-8

(Present-day heroines, Madam Scholars, proponents of tenderness
and beautiful sentiments, I defy at the same time your verse,
romances, letters, billets doux, all your knowledge, and value this
frank and modest ignorance.)

I have mentioned already the influence of some *précieuses* on political matters of the day. It should not be forgotten also that they had
a similar bearing on linguistic matters. Their interest in purifying
and attempting to clarify language is likely to have influenced
theoreticians. Vaugelas, for example, was a regular attender of
Mme de Rambouillet's salon. Moreover, not only were the salons
a forum for debate about sexual and intellectual matters, but they
were also a melting pot for much literary innovation. *La Princesse de
Clèves*, which I mentioned at the beginning of this chapter, very
probably derived from the collaboration of various people in the
salons. Also, through the salons, different genres of writing, such as
the maxim, portrait and conversation gained prominence.

In the next two chapters, I shall deal with aspects which I have
only briefly outlined in this chapter, aspects which are closely
linked to both *honnêteté* and *préciosité*: genre (Chapter 6) and gender
(Chapter 7).

Selected Reading

E. Bury, *Littérature et politesse: l'invention de l'honnête homme* (Paris, 1996). A
good recent study of *honnêteté*, incorporating and commenting on much
other scholarship on the term. In French.

P. France, *Politeness and its Discontents: problems in French classical culture*
(Cambridge, 1992). A collection of disparate essays. Chapter 4 constitutes a cogent discussion of different codes of politeness.

J. Mesnard, *La Culture du XVIIe siècle* (Paris, 1992), pp. 142-159. Some
over-generalized statements mar, otherwise an interesting chapter on
honnêtes gens. In French.

M. Moriarty, *Taste and Ideology in Seventeenth-Century France* (Cambridge,
1988). A subtle and stimulating analysis of the meanings and complexities of the term *goût*, including chapters on Méré, La Rochefoucauld
and La Bruyère.

6

Tensions in Genre

The complexities of *honnêteté* and *préciosité* were shown in the last chapter to play a large role in distinctions of class, religion and gender. So too did they have an influence on the question of genre. Many innovative forms of writing emerged from the salons, some of which I shall examine in this chapter.

Before looking at these different kinds of writing, it is worth considering a seventeenth-century perception of genre, in a work which itself was first read aloud in the salons. In 1674, Boileau published his *Art poétique*, a conscious imitation of the Roman writer Horace's *Ars Poetica*, where he discusses the many different forms of poetry. In Chant III, he follows Horace in considering the great forms: *tragédie* (lines 1-159); *épopée* (epic poetry, lines 160-334) and *comédie* (lines 335-423). As will have been apparent in the first three chapters of this book, tragedy and comedy in the theatre dominated the seventeenth-century French literary world. The King's support of the theatre arose in no small measure from the fact that these genres had been so prominent in ancient classical times. The publicity machine which surrounded Louis XIV wished to depict him as the natural successor to the great Roman emperors (as can be seen in many portraits, engravings and medals from the time), and his endorsement of such genres would only add credence to that image. In Chant II of the *Art poétique*, Boileau analyses the minor genres: *idylle, élégie, ode, sonnet, épigramme, rondeau, ballade, madrigal, satire, vaudeville* and *chanson*.

Of these various poetic forms, there is one interesting omission by Boileau: the fable. Although La Fontaine's first volume of *Fables choisies mises en vers* had appeared in 1668, the fable was evidently still considered an inferior form and not associated with poetry. As I shall argue, the fable, while not incarnating contemporary perceptions of an accepted poetic medium, nonetheless successfully exploits many tensions within the seventeenth century.

In addition to the fable, there are a number of shorter genres which flourished within the milieu of the salons and which challenge the stereotype of the seventeenth century as an age in which large-scale works (such as long prose texts and tragedies) dominated. We shall see how many of these different forms were interrelated. The short format was well suited to an environment where conversation was so important: bite-sized pieces were easier to discuss in short periods than lengthier genres. There was also a vogue for the publication of collections of literary anecdotes, known as *ana*. These *ana* were usually named after prominent personalities of the day. Amongst the better known collections are *Ménagiana*, *Huetiana* and *Segraisiana*. Another form of entertainment in the salons was the solving of enigmas, a form which had been popular in French writings from medieval times.

A number of the shorter genres which I shall discuss in this chapter, like so many of the major seventeenth-century genres, were influenced by classical or ancient sources. The maxim and fragment, for example, can be seen to emanate from such diverse roots as Biblical aphorisms, Roman *sententiae*, the Latin authors Seneca's and Martial's epigrams, and the Stoic philosopher Epictetus' short writings; indeed, the latter three writers were widely translated in seventeenth-century France. The portrait owed much of its popularity to the famous sixteenth-century translation by Amyot of Plutarch's portrait of historical figures. Perhaps the most famous memoirs from ancient times were those of Julius Caesar. The epistolary format played an important role in Ancient Rome, most notably in the works of Cicero. In the sphere of conversation, dialogues were used by, amongst others, Socrates, Cicero and St Augustine. It is significant that, despite the debt which they owed to ancient sources, all these forms were moulded to shape the demands of seventeenth-century salon society and in no way can they be seen simply as imitations.

1. Shorter 'Literary' Forms

a. Fable

Although the fable lacked distinction in France at the time that La Fontaine was writing, as we saw in Boileau's lack of reference to it in his *Art Poétique*, nonetheless the form (like so many of the genres) had illustrious ancient antecedents. As far back as 600 B.C., Aesop was writing fables, many of which were reworked by La Fontaine. Another major influence on him was the Latin writer Phaedrus, whose work had only recently been rediscovered. Phaedrus is significant, as he wrote his fables in verse. La Fontaine modestly claims that in his work 'on ne trouvera pas ici l'élégance ni l'extrême brèveté qui rendent Phèdre recommendable: ce sont qualités au-dessus de ma portée' (you will not find in this work either the elegance or extreme brevity which make Phaedrus such a recommended author: these qualities are above my capabilities). But time has proved that La Fontaine possessed Phaedrus's qualities in abundance.

The fact that La Fontaine's fables have been enjoyed by children ever since the seventeenth century testifies to their popularity as pleasurable tales. But obviously their interest resides in other features. Appearance rarely matches reality. This much used seventeenth-century theme recurs at many points in the *Fables*. In 'Le Lion et le Chasseur' (The Lion and the Huntsman) (Book VI, Fable 2), the poet explicitly applies the theme of appearance and reality to the complexity of the fable:

Les Fables ne sont pas ce qu'elles semblent être.
Le plus simple animal nous y tient lieu de Maître.
Une Morale nue apporte de l'ennui;
Le conte fait passer le précepte avec lui.

En ces sortes de feinte il faut instruire et plaire,
Et conter pour conter me semble peu d'affaire.

(Fables are not what they seem to be. The simplest animal can play
the role of Master. A bare moral provokes boredom. The story
brings the message with it. In these kinds of pretence, one must
teach and entertain, and telling a story simply for the purpose of
telling a story seems pointless to me.)

In the very line that the commonplace reference to the necessity for
the coexistence of instruction and pleasure is made, the poet
readily admits that, although his fables may appear spontaneous
and natural, his task is essentially artificial: it is 'une feinte' (line 5).
But this is precisely what energizes so much of seventeenth-century
literature: the conscious absorption of contradictions. The fable is
nourished on such tensions, where seemingly incompatible aspects
coexist. I will mention just three such seeming incompatibilities.
First, fables are intended to be understood and enjoyed by children
and yet are aimed also at an adult audience. Second, we find the
deliberate juxtaposition of old and new worlds. As La Fontaine
stresses in the Preface, the old tales should be well known to those
who read them, but at the same time 'on veut de la nouveauté'
(novelty is needed). Thirdly, the fable is a form where *vraisemblance*
has no part to play (nobody believes that animals can talk amongst
themselves nor that, as is the case in many of the fables, animals
speak the same language as humans), and yet the whole purpose of
the fable is to discover truths which reside in them.

I shall choose one well-known fable to illustrate these points:

'La Grenouille qui se Veut Faire Aussi Grosse que le Boeuf'

Une Grenouille vit un boeuf
Qui lui sembla de belle taille.
Elle qui n'était pas grosse en tout comme un oeuf
Envieuse s'étend, et s'enfle, et se travaille
Pour égaler l'animal en grosseur,
Disant: Regardez bien, ma soeur;

Est-ce assez? dites-moi; n'y suis-je point encore?
– Nenni. – M'y voici donc? – Point du tout. – M'y voilà?
– Vous n'en approchez point. La chétive pécore
S'enfla si bien qu'elle creva.
Le monde est plein de gens qui ne sont pas plus sages:
Tout Bourgeois veut bâtir comme les grands Seigneurs,
Tout petit Prince a des Ambassadeurs,
Tout Marquis veut avoir des Pages.

Book I, Fable 3

('The Frog who wishes to make herself as big as the ox': A frog saw an ox who seemed to her to be perfectly sized. She was no bigger than an egg, and in a state of envy stretched herself, puffed herself up and worked hard to equal the size of the other animal, saying: Look, my sister, is this enough; am I there yet? – No. – Is this nearer? – Not at all. – Am I there now? – You are not even close. The puny little creature puffed herself up so much that she burst. The world is full of people who are no more wise than this: every bourgeois wants to build houses like great lords, every prince has ambassadors, every marquess wishes to have pages.)

The image of a frog bursting would appeal to the ghoulish fascination of a child (after all, how many reading this would claim in their childhood never to have subjected defenceless insects or animals to some form of cruelty?). Yet at the same time, the informed reader would immediately discern in this image the absurdity of one who strives to be something which he or she is not. Although the story of a frog talking to an ox is obviously implausible, the message which it conveys would strike most readers as plausible. Also, although the tale of animals is timeless, in the final four lines the poet relates the tale to his own contemporary world of bourgeois, princes and marquis.

In order to justify his choice of the fable, La Fontaine compares the moral element of the fable (the *apologue*) to biblical parables in the Preface, adding that truth can best be communicated in this way:

nous voyons que la Vérité a parlé aux hommes par paraboles; et la parabole est-elle autre chose que l'Apologue, c'est-à-dire un exemple fabuleux, et qui s'insinue avec d'autant plus de facilité et d'effet, qu'il est plus commun et plus familier?

(we see that truth has spoken to men through parables; and is the parable anything other than a fable, in other words an imaginary example which insinuates itself with as much ease as effect, which is both more common and more familiar?)

Although in the first half of the sentence he chooses not to discern any difference between the relative status of religious truth and the truth contained within his fables, a disparity is immediately apparent in the following verb ('s'insinuer'), hardly appropriate to denote sacred truth, and nouns ('facilité' and 'effet'), implying above all theatrical effect.

Another ramification of the noun 'effet' is that the reader/listener/spectator is inextricably implicated. In other words, without any reader response there can be no effect. To sum up the effect of the fable, therefore, it is to a large extent the reader who derives from the fable whatever level of truth or enjoyment he or she chooses.

b. Maxim

If we take into account the late eighteenth century/ early nineteenth century maxim writer Joseph Joubert's definition of a maxim, there might seem to be a similar lack of distinction between different kinds of truth as in La Fontaine's view of the fable: 'Une maxime est l'expression exacte et noble d'une vérité importante et incontestable. Les bonnes maximes sont les germes de tout bien; fortement imprimées dans la mémoire, elles nourrissent la volonté' (A maxim is the precise and noble expression of an important and incontestable truth. Good maxims are the germs of all that is good; firmly imprinted in the memory, they nourish the will). However, as we shall find with the example of La Rochefoucauld, more is at stake with the seventeenth-century maxim than the expression of an unambiguous truth.

Maxim-writers preferred to see themselves as *moralistes*. The term *moraliste* is defined by the Furetière dictionary as 'auteur qui écrit, qui traite de la morale' (an author who writes about and considers morality), and in its turn 'morale' is defined as 'la doctrine des moeurs' (the doctrine of social mores). In other words, there is a great difference between a 'moraliste' (moralist), whose task is primarily descriptive, and a 'moralisateur' (moralizer), whose role is above all prescriptive. While the 'moraliste' attempts not to make rulings on how we should behave, the 'moralisateur' has a preordained agenda, perhaps religious, philosophical or political.

The popularity of the maxim in the salons of the time came from the delight which was taken in virtuosic displays of linguistic skill. Significantly, all the prominent maxim-writers of the time, such as La Rochefoucauld, Mme de Sablé and the abbé d'Ailly, frequented the literary salons. Maxims would be read aloud in these circles and commented upon. Their initial impact would therefore have been poetic: the sound of the words and their clever juxtaposition would impress before their meaning was imbibed. To take an example from Mme de Sablé's *Maximes*:

> Etre trop mécontent de soi est une faiblesse. Etre trop content de soi est une sottise. (5)

> (To be too discontent with oneself is weakness. To be too content with oneself is stupidity.)

Our initial response to this maxim is to remark upon the perfect symmetry of the two sentences. We then notice the juxtaposition in each sentence of opposing adjectives and nouns: 'mécontent' and 'content'; 'faiblesse' and 'sottise'. Only after these impressions do we consider the significance of the meaning.

It follows then that the form of the maxim suggests self-enclosure and completeness. There are no redundant words. Nothing is left open-ended. Considering the completeness of the form, it would seem unlikely that tensions would exist. Yet, if we look at La Rochefoucauld, we find that at no point does he question the status of language:

> Il y a des faussetés déguisées qui représentent si bien la vérité que ce serait mal juger que de ne s'y pas laisser tromper. (282)

> (There are disguised falsities which represent truth so well that it would be bad judgement not to be deceived by them.)

On the surface, he appears to make a distinction between different terms, such as between 'faussetés' and 'vérité' here, thereby implicitly accepting the clarity of the terms; but the very fact that he does not define his understanding of what the terms mean, we as readers are left in an ambiguous position. How are we to distinguish between 'faussetés déguisées' and 'la vérité'? For all we know, what we take to be the truth is in fact a disguised falsehood. Or, perhaps even more worryingly, we may discern as false what is really true. Moreover, could this nugget of 'truth' which is being offered to us here by the maxim-writer be itself a carefully disguised falsehood? The use of verbs like 'déguiser' and 'représenter' only adds to the reader's instability. So much in the seventeenth century is about performance and disguise, as we shall find even more tellingly in the following chapter on Gender.

The notion of disguise and moral complexity permeates much of the *Maximes*, especially as it is signalled at the very beginning of the collection in the maxim which La Rochefoucauld chose as the epigraph to the work:

> Nos vertus ne sont le plus souvent que des vices déguisés.

> (Our virtues are the most often only disguised vices.)

As with truth and falsity, we are given no clear direction as to how to distinguish between vice and virtue. The words 'le plus souvent' only serve to confuse the issue further, because if, following the dictum of the epigraph, we choose to distrust the appearance of virtue, there will be times when our scepticism is misplaced. The disparity between word and thing is further underlined by another maxim concerned with virtue and vice:

> Le nom de la vertu sert à l'intérêt aussi utilement que les vices. (187)

> (The name 'virtue' serves personal interest as usefully as vices.)

There is no way of differentiating between the word that is 'vertu' and actual virtue. The fact that the word can assist one's self-interest destabilizes the concept even further. This theme of self-interest, or *amour-propre*, is central to both La Rochefoucauld's and Pascal's thought and has been linked in both cases to the influence of St Augustine in the circles which they frequented, although it would be fair to say that Augustine's ethical perspective of self-love (as the antithesis of the love of God) is closer to Pascal's outlook than to La Rochefoucauld's more secular application of the term.

When the *Maximes* were first published, contemporary reaction was that of bewilderment. The lack of a firm authorial voice was seen to give the maxims an uneasy ambiguity. Even friends such as Mme de Liancourt, while praising them, suggested some changes:

> ... je vois bien qu'il y a dans ce manuscrit de fort jolies choses, pourvu qu'on ôte l'équivoque qui fait confondre les vraies vertus avec les fausses.

> (... I can see some very beautiful things in this manuscript, provided that one eliminates the ambiguity which confuses true virtues with false ones.)

As will be apparent from the few maxims which I have examined, the concision of the maxim allows for many tensions which cannot be resolved. The careful arrangement of words makes those words, as in a poem, more readily memorable, but we as readers are given no direction as to how to interpret them. Paradoxically, this is both emprisoning and liberating for the reader. On the one hand, he or she is seduced by the poetic patterning of the words and therefore is emprisoned within an appreciation of verbal dexterity, which has little to do with grasping the meaning of the maxim. On the other hand, the lack of elucidation as to how we should distinguish between these absolute concepts gives the reader the freedom to make sense of the maxim by him or herself. In other words, the reader is actively involved in the creative process of the maxim, because each individual interpretation will invariably be different. Moreover, by trying to understand the meaning of contradictory concepts, the reader is trying to comprehend the wider moral implications of living within society.

Both the fact that maxims were read aloud in the salons and the theme of disguise in La Rochefoucauld's *Maximes* show that even this most succinct of forms contains an element of theatricality. Indeed, maxims themselves appear in theatre of the day. At times, a character uses maxim-like statements to impose moral authority upon other characters, such as when Agnès is forced by Arnolphe to read out the 'Maximes du Mariage' in Molière's *L'Ecole des femmes* (Act III, scene 2) or when Mme Pernelle lists what she considers to be the immoral activities of her son's family in Molière's *Tartuffe* (Act I, scene 1). In many of Corneille's plays, where moral conflicts predominate, characters often exchange maxims while attempting to gain the upper hand in debates.

La Bruyère's *Caractères* have often been compared to La Rochefoucauld's *Maximes* in that they also contain short statements on human nature and morality. However, in his Preface, La Bruyère is keen to distance himself from being viewed simply as a maxim-writer. Interestingly, he equates maxims with prescriptive intent and attempts to explain the diverging length of his pieces as being formed specially to suit differing subjects. Whereas the form of the maxim dictates to a large extent the moral elusiveness of its subject matter, La Bruyère claims that form is subservient to content:

> Ce ne sont point au reste des maximes que j'aie voulu écrire: elles
> sont comme des lois dans la morale, et j'avoue que je n'ai ni assez

d'autorité ni assez de génie pour faire le législateur: je sais même
que j'aurais péché contre l'usage des maximes, qui veut qu'à la
manière des oracles elles soient courtes et concises; quelques-unes
de ces remarques le sont, quelques autres sont plus étendues: on
pense les choses d'une manière différente et on les explique par un
tour aussi tout différent, par une sentence, par un raisonnement,
par une métaphore ou quelque autre figure, par un parallèle, par
une simple comparaison, par un fait tout entier, par un seul trait,
par une description, par une peinture: de là procède la longueur ou
la brièveté de mes réflexions.

(I did not want to write maxims: they are like moral laws, and I
admit that I have neither the authority nor aptitude to play the
legislator; I know even that I would have contradicted the purpose
of maxims, which demands that in an oracle-like way they should
be short and concise; some of the remarks which follow are indeed
short, some others are longer: one thinks of things differently and
so one explains them differently, in a sententia, a piece of reasoning,
a metaphor or other kind of figure, a parallel, a simple comparison,
a complete fact, a single trait, a description, a portrait; the length or
brevity of my thoughts proceeds from there.)

Just as we saw that La Rochefoucauld's *Maximes* are paradoxically
liberating due to the freedom given to the reader, La Bruyère's
comments here dictate against the stereotype of the seventeenth
century as inflexible. He allows through the diversity of form for
freedom of thought, which again gives the reader versatility in his
or her interpretation of texts. According to him, no form is static,
and he modulates that form in his *Caractères* to suit his subject-matter. Therefore, whereas we find many examples of La Rochefou-
cauldesque maxims, such as 'La moquerie est souvent indigence
d'esprit' (mockery is often laziness of mind) (V, 57), we also find
long passages devoted to the extended discussion of humanity and
his contemporaries in particular.

c. Fragment

Whereas the maxim is self-enclosed, the fragment (whether deliberately or not) is open-ended. Its very incompletion calls for the reader to make sense of the text in a way different from that of reading the maxim, to look beyond the lacunae which inevitably exist.

Pascal's *Pensées*, perhaps the most celebrated fragmentary work of the seventeenth century, was left incomplete at the time of his death in 1662. Most critics in the past have attributed the work's fragmentary state to Pascal's inability to complete the project. As early as 1670, when the first edition appeared, the Port-Royal editors apologized for its apparent inconsistencies, and ever since subsequent editors and critics have attempted to reconstitute Pascal's intended order for the *Pensées*. Although some chapter headings for the work exist, ultimately such a reconstitution is only speculative, as we shall never know either his exact intentions or what changes he might subsequently have made if he had lived longer. On the other hand, Pascal's own words on disorder seem to offer more valuable clues to the possibility that fragmentation would have played a very important role in the completed project. Indeed, the lack of order of thoughts would seem to be fundamental to his persuasive purpose:

> J'écrirai ici mes pensées sans ordre et non pas peut-être dans une confusion sans dessein. C'est le véritable ordre et qui marquera toujours mon objet par le désordre même. Je ferais trop d'honneur à mon sujet si je le traitais avec ordre puisque je veux montrer qu'il en est incapable.
>
> *Pensées*, Lafuma 532

> (I shall write my thoughts here in no particular order but not perhaps in a confusion which lacks design. That is the true order, which will always mark out my objective through disorder. I would be paying too much respect to my subject-matter if I treated it in an ordered way since I want to show precisely that it is incapable of order.)

Random disorder is clearly not being advocated here: his thoughts will be written in a disordered way which is not 'sans dessein'. As we saw in Chapter 4, the doctrine of the corruption of mankind after the Fall is central to the *Pensées*. A fragmentary text would be the most effective way of acting as a continual reminder to the reader of his or her corrupt and disordered state. But, even more crucially, as we saw with the maxim, the reader is given the freedom to make sense of the fragments. Pascal emphasizes this in another fragment where he claims that, although his subject-matter may not be entirely original, its ordering (*disposition*) is new:

> Qu'on ne dise pas que je n'ai rien dit de nouveau, la disposition des matières est nouvelle. Quand on joue à la paume c'est une même balle dont joue l'un et l'autre, mais l'un la place mieux.
>
> Pensées, Lafuma 696
>
> (Let no-one say that I have said nothing new; the ordering of the material is new. When one plays tennis each player uses the same ball, but one places it better than the other.)

The choice of the tennis metaphor is particularly apt. While trying to outwit an opponent on the tennis court, a player places the ball in unexpected places. Similarly, we as readers are being kept alert by reading fragments in unexpected parts of the text. Unlike in the *Maximes*, where we know that we will be reading for the most part pithy statements, Pascal ranges from maxim-like statements to longer passages to deliberately truncated or incomplete statements. A brief fragment like 'Condition de l'homme. Inconstance, Ennui, Inquiétude' (Man's Condition. Inconstancy, Ennui, Anxiety) (*Pensées*, Lafuma 24), for example, cannot be termed a maxim. It remains open-ended, inviting us to look beyond the list of nouns to explore by ourselves elsewhere in the text (where the three terms figure prominently) what precisely is meant by these concepts. Even the status of language is continually called into question. To take just one example, the image of watching moving objects from a stationary position and vice versa is exploited to show how with words we are similarly unstable:

> Ceux qui sont dans le dérèglement disent à ceux qui sont dans l'ordre que ce sont eux qui s'éloignent de la nature et ils la croient suivre, comme ceux qui sont dans un vaisseau croient que ceux qui sont au bord fuient. Le langage est pareil de tous côtés.
>
> *Pensées*, 697

> (Those in a state of disorder tell those whose lives are ordered that it is the ordered ones who are unnatural; they by contrast think they are following nature, just as those in a boat think that it is those on the shore who are moving. Language is similar in all aspects.)

At no point in the text are we allowed to attain a sense of complacency. Tensions are exploited in order to persuade the reader both to acknowledge his or her instability and to search beyond the immediate fragmentary text for a greater certainty, which is incarnated for Pascal in the Christian God.

The short format is therefore evidently one which contradicts so many stereotypes of the seventeenth century. The comment by the eighteenth-century writer abbé Trublet perhaps best sums up how the short form transformed the relationship between reader and text:

> Un Lecteur, homme d'esprit et de réflexion, devient Auteur, en lisant Pascal, La Rochefoucauld, La Bruyère …
>
> 'Sur la manière d'écrire par pensées détachées', *Essais sur divers sujets de littérature et de morale*, 1735, p. 9.

> (A reader, who is both intelligent and reflective, becomes an author when reading Pascal, La Rochefoucauld and La Bruyère …)

d. Portrait

All three authors mentioned by Trublet can be linked in differing ways to the popularity in the seventeenth century of the literary portrait. La Rochefoucauld wrote several portraits himself, and pieces like '*Peinture de l'amour-propre*' (published in 1660) can be seen as significant transitions from the vogue for the portrait to his own growing interest in the maxim. The portrait of various figures in La Bruyère's *Caractères* shows the strong influence of earlier literary portraits. Pascal, by contrast, was severely critical of self-portraiture, perhaps most famously in his condemnation of Montaigne's 'sot projet ... de se peindre' (stupid project of painting his own portrait, *Pensées*, Lafuma 780), as he saw this as evidence of man's inflated preoccupation with the self.

1659 represents the year in which the portrait was at the height of its popularity (and it is no coincidence that this corresponds exactly with the period of the popularity of *préciosité*), as two major collections of portraits were published. Before that, Madeleine de Scudéry and her brother Georges had helped to raise the status of the portrait in their works, especially the fifth part of *Clélie*.

The definition of the portrait at the end of the century by Richelet shows both the versatility of its form and the similarities in its concern with social mores between the portrait and the maxim:

> Le Portrait est une description grave, enjouée, ou satirique de quelque personne. Il a pour matière le corps, l'esprit, les vertus, ou les vices. Son caractère est fleuri, et naturel. On fait le portrait en vers, ou en prose; ou bien en vers et en prose tout ensemble. Les choses s'y tournent d'une manière à inspirer de l'estime, de l'amour, ou de la haine: et l'on travaille à y marquer naturellement l'air, le visage, les moeurs et les inclinations des gens. L'une de ses plus sensibles beautés consiste en cela. Il ne faut pourtant pas peindre si fort d'après-nature, qu'on n'aille un peu au-delà; mais sans choquer la vraisemblance. Les grands Peintres le pratiquent de la sorte; et on doit les imiter.
>
> *Les Plus Belles Lettres françaises*, 1698, vol. 1, pp. 187-8.

(The Portrait is a description of some person, sometimes serious, light-hearted or satirical. Its subject matter concerns body, mind, virtues or vices. Its character is both flowery and natural. Portraits are written in verse or in prose or even in both verse and prose together. Everything in it is shaped so as to inspire respect, love or even hatred, and writers work hard to depict in a natural way the behaviour, face, character and preferences of people, which is one of its most apparent beauties. However, one must not paint so close to nature so as not to go further, as long as it maintains plausibility. The great painters do it this way, and they should be imitated.)

Interest in the literary portrait arose directly from an attempt to emulate the painted portrait, where there was much debate concerning the representation of likeness or the deliberate improvement or distortion of a face. In literature of the time, painted portraits play a significant role. In *La Princesse de Clèves*, for example, the portraits of Nemours and the princess are crucial to the evolving love of the two protagonists for each other. In many ways, the literary portrait was a short-lived fashion, which followed its own conventions. But, significantly, as we have already seen with La Rochefoucauld, La Bruyère and Pascal, it was a form which concerned many central figures of the day. Molière, for example, includes a portrait scene in *Le Misanthrope* (Act II, scene 4), where the character Célimène ruthlessly satirizes people of her acquaintance. Others, such as Mme de Lafayette and Mme de Sévigné both participated fully in writing and being described in portraits.

Perhaps the most significant feature of the portrait is that, as conventional a form as it was, it consituted an acute commentary on the society which it was describing. Also, in a world where politeness, rules and *bienséances* were all-important, the portrait provided an opportunity to escape from the rigid rules of form and behaviour by which literary society seemed to be governed. Some self-portraitists provided acute analysis of their strengths and foibles while other portraitists were able (like Célimène) to provide cutting critiques of people from their society. Moreover, it gave some people the freedom to express their reaction against the rigid rules of society and particularly religion. One self-portrait by the Chevalier de Lignières shows both his sense of autonomy and religious freedom, which could not so easily have been expressed in other genres. Indeed, one can almost imagine Molière's Dom Juan proclaiming the following words:

> La lecture a rendu mon Esprit assez fort
> Contre toutes les peurs que l'on a de la Mort,
> Et ma Religion n'a rien qui m'embarrasse
> Je me ris du scrupule, et je hais la grimace;
> Quoique je n'aime pas à prier nuit et jour
> Les heureux habitants du céleste séjour,
> Je ne prétendrais pas avoir l'Ame moins bonne,
> Et je ne voudrais pas faire tort à personne.
>
> *Recueil des portraits et éloges*, 1659, p. 333

(Reading has strengthened my mind against one's fears of death, and my religion is not at all embarrassing. I laugh at religious scruples and hate the outward show of them. Although I do not like praying night and day to the happy inhabitants of the celestial resting place, I would not claim to have a soul which is less good, and I would not wish to wrong anyone.)

e. Memoir

A natural extension of the portrait is the memoir, which was a popular form in the seventeenth century. Many memoirs contain several portraits of contemporary figures. Bussy-Rabutin, for example, who is renowned for the malicious portrait of his cousin Mme de Sévigné, included a number of portraits in his *Mémoires* of figures such as Conti, Turenne and Mazarin.

In many ways, the memoir represents an amalgamation of many forms, some of which feature in this chapter. A major influence, as I have shown already in other spheres, came from the previous century in the *Essais* of Montaigne, which symbolized the ideal form of confessional text written for *honnêtes gens*. Spiritual confessional works, such as lives of saints, were also popular in the seventeenth century. The memoirs of Mademoiselle de Montpensier, for example, reflect the influence of such texts. Another dominant confessional text was St Augustine's *Confessions*, which was translated by Robert Arnauld d'Andilly in the century and which is reflected in the writings of many authors associated with Port-Royal, such as Pascal, Antoine Arnauld and Pierre Nicole. The fact that autobiographical memoirs tended to be written towards the end of the authors' lives links the memoir to two other forms, the *éloge* (eulogy) and the *oraison funèbre* (funeral oration), both of which are concerned with retrospective analysis. Letters and conversation also play important roles in memoirs, the former through their significance as documentary evidence, the latter acting as the model for the intimate and seemingly spontaneous style of the memoir.

The most prominent memoir writer recalling the seventeenth century is technically from the eighteenth century. The voluminous *Mémoires* of Saint-Simon (1675-1755) contain, amongst other ages, a retrospective analysis of the last years of Louis XIV's reign, juxtaposing formal accounts of ceremonial occasions and seemingly spontaneous observations of everyday occurrences. In many ways he epitomizes the variety and paradoxicality of the age.

f. Sermon

I have mentioned already that at the beginning of 'De la chaire' in his *Caractères*, La Bruyère notes that 'le discours chrétien est devenu un spectacle' (the Christian sermon has become a theatrical spectacle). This comment not only shows the increasing theatricality of sermons in the seventeenth century. It also reveals their great drawing power. Mme de Sévigné writes often of her favourite preachers, especially the Jesuit Père Bourdaloue, whose popularity was widespread. In a letter written on the 13 March 1671, for example, Mme de Sévigné tells her daughter of a sermon by Bourdaloue as if it were a society event: 'Tout ce qui est au monde était à ce sermon, et ce sermon était digne de tout ce qui l'écoutait' (everybody who is anybody was at this sermon, and it was worthy of all those who heard it).

Along with this fashion for hearing sermons came published sermons. Already in the first half of the century, the published sermons of Jean-Pierre Camus (who was by far the most prolific and the most reprinted author of sermons of the time) and Etienne Molinier were especially popular. By the second half of the century, there were many preachers of note. In addition to Bourdaloue, the names of Fléchier and Massillon figure prominently. The most celebrated printed sermons must be Bossuet's *Oraisons funèbres.* The funeral oration had become prevalent in the century after the death of Henri IV in 1610. Bossuet perfected the form in his orations upon the deaths of leading personalities like Henriette de France (1669), Henriette d'Angleterre (1670), Marie-Thérèse d'Autriche (1683) and the prince de Condé (1687).

2. 'Non-Literary' Forms

a. Letter

Coexistent with the prominence of printed sermons was the vogue for spiritual letters. François de Sales (1567-1622), whose manuals on religious life were most influential, wrote many letters, 2100 of which appear in his *Oeuvres complètes.* Subsequently, volumes of letters became an integral part of seventeenth-century spiritual life.

Although the letter would appear to be simply a personal communication from one person to another, and therefore essentially non-literary, during the seventeenth century fictional letters began to play an increasingly important role. The use of fictional personae and the epistolary format in Pascal's *Lettres provinciales,* which I discussed in Chapter 4, are essential to the satire and polemic of the Jansenist-Jesuit debate. Another epistolary work, the *Lettres portugaises* (1669), for long assumed to be genuine letters from a Portuguese nun to her French lover who had deserted her, is now generally accepted to be the fictional work of Guilleragues (1628-85). Mme de Sévigné refers to them in her real letters, using the term 'portugaises' to signify tender letters (19 July 1671 and 23 January 1682). Despite the obvious discrepancies between fictional and non-fictional letters, there is also a definite connection to be made between them. As Geneviève Haroche-Bouzinac puts it in her book on the epistolary form, *L'épistolaire*, 'le jeu sur destinataire implicite et destinataire explicite existe aussi bien dans la lettre "réelle" que dans la lettre "fictive" et "de fiction" ' (the play on an implicit and explicit addressee exists as much in 'real' letters as in 'fictitious' or 'fictional' letters) (p. 143).

In Mme de Sévigné's letters, her most frequent correspondent – her daughter, Mme de Grignan – is idealized, almost fictionalized. She even compares her daughter (16 May 1672) to the heroine of a novel. This 'fictionalization' is due partly to the obsessive love of mother for daughter. An often difficult relationship in the flesh became idealized as a perfect bond in Mme de Sévigné's letters during the frequent periods that the two were absent from each other, when Mme de Sévigné remained in Paris and her daughter lived with her husband in Provence. Moreover, many of the letters are written in order to entertain her daughter, to keep her attention and good will. She therefore creates her own rhetorical framework, designed for the entertainment of her privileged correspondent. The sense of fiction is also exacerbated by the fact that Mme de Grignan's letters to her mother have not survived, and so we as modern readers only have the single authorial voice of Mme de Sévigné. We can only imagine through references to Mme de Grignan's letters what was contained in them.

Moreover, as spontaneous or as natural as her letters may appear to be, she displays throughout her correspondence a strong awareness of artfulness. Her view of society is often theatricalized, made into a dramatic scenario of her own making. I shall choose one example, concerning the illness of her friend Mme de Brissac:

> Mme de Brissac avait aujourd'hui la colique. Elle était au lit, belle et coiffée à coiffer tout le monde. Je voudrais que vous eussiez vu ce qu'elle faisait de ses douleurs, et l'usage qu'elle faisait de ses yeux, et des cris, et des bras, et des mains qui traînaient sur sa couverture, et les situations, et la compassion qu'elle voulait qu'on eût. Chamarrée de tendresse et d'admiration, j'admirai cette pièce et je la trouvai si belle, que mon attention a dû paraître un saisissement dont je crois qu'on me saura bon gré. [...] Quand je songe avec

quelle simplicité vous êtes malade, le repos que vous donnez à votre joli visage, et enfin quelle différence! cela me paraît plaisant. Au reste, je mange mon potage de la main gauche; c'est une nouveauté.

21 May 1676

(Mme de Brissac had colic today. She was in bed, beautiful and bonneted in the most sumptuous fashion. I wish you could have seen what she made of her pains, and the use of her eyes, and the cries, and the arms, and the hands which trailed over her bed-clothes, and the poses, and the compassion which she wanted us to have. Overcome with tenderness and admiration, I admired this performance and I found it so beautiful that my close attentiveness must have appeared like deep emotion which I think will be much appreciated. ... When I think of the simplicity with which you are ill, the peace which you give to your pretty face, what a difference! it seems so amusing. Apart from this, I am eating my soup with my left hand. It's quite a novelty.)

This account functions on four main levels. The first concerns Mme de Brissac's appearance; some spectators might believe her to be truly ill. On the second level, we find the role played by Mme de Brissac of somebody ill, and observed by Mme de Sévigné, whose use of polysyndeton (several conjunctions in a single sentence) only serves to accentuate the accumulation of gestures which Mme de Brissac makes use of in order to reinforce the effect of her performance. The third level comprises also a theatrical perform-ance, but this time it is Mme de Sévigné's role as concerned spectator, interpreted by all as a sincere reaction. On the fourth level, Mme de Sévigné as a genuine spectator admires Mme de Brissac's theatrical performance; it is surely no coincidence that her use of the terms 'compassion' and 'admiration' reflects the vocabulary of tragic effect widely used by her favourite dramatist, Pierre Corneille. At first it seems that Mme de Sévigné's sub-sequent comparison of Mme de Brissac's illness with that of her daughter is evoked to demonstrate the affectation of the former and the natural simplicity of the latter. But this reading would inevitably undermine the positive force which Mme de Sévigné accords to every kind of theatricality. We find described here two different theatrical performances: the first is Mme de Brissac's performance, heroic, larger than life, of a Cornelian grandeur; the second is Mme de Grignan's performance, moving, calm, of a Racinian simplicity, but none the less a performance. Note the words, 'le repos que vous *donnez* à votre joli visage', which imply that even simplicity has a theatrical side. No matter how natural Mme de Sévigné's style may appear to be, we should not forget that that spontaneity is not without artifice. Theatricality for Mme de Sévigné forms therefore an integral part of each aspect of life. This idea is underlined at the end of the letter on Mme de Brissac. Although she may well be referring to the rhumatism from which she suffered, she overthrows any notion of naturalness by applying the word 'nouveauté' to her decision to eat her soup with her left hand. In so doing, she gives the impression both that she is mocking the affectations and fashions of her age and subverting any idea that she may be upholding natural values in opposition to the artifice of Mme de Brissac.

Some critics have attempted to stress the spontaneity (and by implication the artlessness) of Mme de Sévigné's letters by referring to her own description of her letters as conversations. As we have already seen in this book, conversation was the starting point and *raison d'être* of many art forms and movements in the seventeenth century. A short consideration of the conversation as an art form itself may help to dispel all notion of Mme de Sévigné's correspondence as artless.

b. Conversation

Conversation and dialogue were evidently central to the salons and to the seventeenth century in general, not simply providing the forum for frothy subjects to be discussed. Indeed, conversation was evidently regarded as worthy of serious respect. Guez de Balzac, for example, writes of the necessity for 'une Histoire de la Conversation' (a History of Conversation), and Mlle de Scudéry in her

Conversations sur de divers sujets (1680) even suggests the need for 'des règles de la conversation' (rules for conversation).

With the importance of dialogue, conversation was integral to genres such as the theatre and the novel. But it also plays a part in works on religion, especially those concerned with spiritual direction. One example, Pascal's *Entretien avec M. de Sacy*, documents the conversations which Pascal had with his spiritual director. Moreover, education theories of the time at Port-Royal were founded upon the importance of dialogue, as opposed to books. One such educationalist, Pierre Coustel, emphasizes the role of conversation in his *Règles pour l'éducation des enfants* (Rules for the education of children, published in 1687):

> il faut toujours, autant qu'on peut, joindre la conférence des hommes savants avec la lecture des bons auteurs, puisqu'on apprend avec bien moins de peine, et plus agréablement ce qu'on ne sait pas, en conférant avec les vivants, qu'en s'entretenant dans son cabinet avec les morts: et l'on voit aussi par une heureuse expérience, que ces sortes d'entretiens polissent l'esprit, forment le jugement, et perfectionnent merveilleusement un jeune homme en très-peu de temps.
>
> 1745 edition, vol. 2, pp. 213-4

> (one must always combine as much as possible the conversation of learned men with reading good authors, since one learns more enjoyably and with less trouble what one does not know by discussing with living people rather than sitting in one's room talking to dead people. And through happy experience, one can see also that these kinds of conversation cultivate the mind, fashion one's judgement and in a marvellous way perfect a young man in very little time.)

A number of treatises and manuals on conversation were published in the second half of the century, including René Bary's *Esprit de cour ou les conversations galantes divisées en cent dialogues* (1662) and Pierre Ortigue de Vaumorière's *Art de plaire dans la conversation* (1688). That champion of *honnêteté*, the Chevalier de Méré himself wrote a collection of prose works entitled *Les Conversations* (1668), and La Bruyère included a chapter in his *Caractères*, entitled 'De la société et de la conversation', where good conversation is clearly regarded both as difficult to achieve and easy to become too contrived:

> C'est une grande misère que de n'avoir pas assez d'esprit pour bien parler, ni assez de jugement pour se taire. Voilà le principe de toute impertinence. (V, 18)

> (It is terribly wretched to have neither enough wit to speak well nor enough good judgement to be silent. That is the principle of every impertinence.)

> Il ne faut pas qu'il y ait trop d'imagination dans nos conversations ni dans nos écrits: elle ne produit souvent que des idées vaines et puériles [...]. (V, 17)

> (One should not have too much imagination in either our conversations or our writings, for it often produces only vain and puerile ideas.)

Other successful works which use the conversation format are Bouhours's *Entretiens d'Ariste et d'Eugène* (1671) and Fontenelle's *Entretiens sur la pluralité des mondes* (1681), the latter of which was a much published work of scientific popularization.

In the last chapter, I mentioned the *Recueil de choses diverses*, a collection of conversations which took place at the hôtel de Liancourt. Unlike the works which I have discussed above, which are largely self-conscious attempts to imitate or to analyse the conversational style, the *Recueil* consists of transcribed conversations which actually took place. They offer fascinating perspectives on what people of the time were talking about in the seventeenth century. Saint-Evremond (1613-1703), who was well known for his witty conversation and a scattering of essays, letters and verse, as well as three comedies, is one such person whose opinions on Corneille and Racine are recorded:

St-Evremond, gentilhomme normand très habile, [...] dit que
Corneille est le seul des poètes qui ait bien connu les qualités d'un
héros et que Racine devrait aller à son école.

p. 375

(St Evremond, a very able Norman gentleman, says that Corneille
is the only poet to have known the qualities of a hero and that
Racine should go to his school.)

In the same collection of conversations, Montaigne's great popularity in the seventeenth century is backed up by the following
remark. Perhaps more surprising in this age of self-congratulation
dominated by the glorious reign of Louis XIV is the criticism by
comparison with Montaigne of writing of the time:

Montaigne est en vogue à présent. Il y a peu de bons auteurs
français: Montaigne est des principaux.

p. 429

(Montaigne is presently in vogue. There are few good French
authors. Montaigne is one of the best.)

*

A number of conclusions can usefully be drawn from this analysis
of different genres. One is that of the interreferentiality of all these
genres and indeed of the more conventional poetic and theatrical
genres: for example, the maxim emanates from the salons but is
also used in the theatre; there is a close relationship between the
maxim and the fragment; literary figures of the day either used or
reacted against the portrait; and there is much commentary on
other genres in both letters and conversations. A second conclusion
is the extent to which all these forms are governed not only by their
own conventions but also by the tensions within and generated by
them. A third conclusion is the prominent role of women in the
salons as positive creative forces, in many cases responding against
the restraints of society beyond the confines of the salon. I will

develop this question of gender in the next chapter, exploring not only the role of women but also the wider spectrum of sexuality.

Further Reading

P. Bayley, *French Pulpit Oratory 1598-1650* (Cambridge, 1980). Useful both for the study of the rhetoric of sermons and a catalogue of printed sermons from the period.

J. Culler, 'Paradox and the Language of Morals in La Rochefoucauld', *Modern Language Review* 68 (1973), pp. 28-39. A challenging article on La Rochefoucauld's use of language.

P. Dandrey, *La Fabrique des fables: essai sur la poétique de La Fontaine* (Paris, 1991). An intelligent discussion of all aspects of La Fontaine's poetic output. In French.

N. Hammond, *Playing with Truth: language and the human condition in Pascal's Pensées* (Oxford, 1994).

G. Haroche-Bouzinac, *L'Épistolaire* (Paris, 1995). A short section on the seventeenth-century letter. In French.

J. Lesaulnier, ed., *Port-Royal insolite: édition critique du Recueil de choses diverses* (Paris, 1992). A fascinating edition of conversations, with comprehensive notes. In French.

E. Lesne, *La Poétique des mémoires (1650-1685)* (Paris, 1996). A detailed analysis of the theory of the memoir. In French.

J. Plantié, *La Mode du portrait littéraire en France 1641-1681* (Paris, 1994). Important for its demonstration of the importance of the portrait not only in the literary salons but in all seventeenth-century genres. In French.

C. Strosetzki, *Rhétorique de la conversation* (Paris, 1987). Excellent analysis of the conversation. In French.

7

Tensions in Gender

On the surface, seventeenth-century France represents the patriarchal state par excellence. On the political stage, the King was perceived as Father of the State. Within the family, the father maintained complete control (as can be seen in the role of the father in many Molière plays). In the theatre, Pierre Corneille supports to a large extent this sense of male domination, praising 'les passions plus mâles [...] que l'amour' (passions which are more masculine than love), where duty to the State takes precedence over matters of the heart.

However, this notion of the all-embracing patriarchal society does not allow for the complexities which lie both below and on the surface. To take a simple example, if we consider the two foremost tragic dramatists of the century, Corneille and Racine, an immediate disparity in the roles played by men and women is apparent. While the eponymous heroes of Corneille are in the greater part men (as shown in plays like *Le Cid*, *Horace*, *Cinna* and *Polyeucte*), the equivalent title parts in Racine's plays are mostly women (such as *Andromaque*, *Bérénice*, *Iphigénie*, *Phèdre*, *Esther* and *Athalie*). Even those Racinian plays where men are the eponymous heroes, such as *Britannicus* and *Bajazet*, female characters tend to dominate: Agrippine in the former and Roxane in the latter. Moreover, the one subject which both Corneille and Racine treated at the same time, that of Bérénice, shows the difference of emphasis placed on the central figures. Whereas Corneille chose to call his version *Tite et Bérénice*, Racine named his simply *Bérénice*. We have seen in earlier chapters how Corneille rebelled against many of the impositions

which were placed upon him. Although many of his female characters act as powerful counterparts to male roles, his tragedies (with
their preoccupations with heroism, duty and *gloire*) tend to conclude with the male-dominated ethos. We shall see later how one
of his comedies transgresses boundaries of gender and sexuality.

1. Women

In Chapter 5, on *honnêteté* and *préciosité*, I discussed the sense of
autonomy which the salons gave to women. While blatant inequal-
ity in perception of the different roles of men and women remained, writers such as Du Bosc in *L'Honnête Femme* (1632) were
keen to stress that women should have 'le courage de rentrer dans
leurs droits' (the courage to discover their rights). More women
than ever before were encouraged to write, and the question of
equal education for women became a burning question throughout the century.

However, not surprisingly, there still remained strong opposition to the greater freedom of women, and it is worth repeating that
much of the hostility towards the *précieuses* undoubtedly came from
resentment towards their proclamations of greater autonomy.

Even before women attained prominence in the salons, a debate
raged about their role in society. In 1617, Alexis Trousset published his *Alphabet de l'imperfection et malice des femmes* (Alphabet of the
imperfection and malice of women), which provoked a vigorous
exchange of refutations and counter-refutations (some 20 works
were published between 1617 and 1629). Amongst the refutations
was Marie de Gournay's *Egalité des hommes et des femmes* (1622).
Marie de Gournay was an early champion of Montaigne's writings, and he had entrusted her with the definitive edition of the
Essais. Her condemnation of Trousset includes a strong assertion
of the equality of the sexes:

> La pluspart de ceux qui prennent la cause des femmes, contre cette
> orgueilleuse preferance que les hommes s'attribuent, leur rendent

le change entier: r'envoyans la preferance vers elles. Moy qui fuys toutes extremitez, je me contente de les esgaler aux hommes: la nature s'opposant pour ce regard autant à la superiorité qu'à l'inferiorité.

p. 61

(Most of those who take up the cause of women against that proud preference which men attribute to themselves turn it round completely, redirecting the preference towards women. I steer clear of all extremes and am happy to find men and women equal, with nature finding each one equally superior as inferior in this regard.)

The question of education is fundamental to her argument. Women were not accorded the same educational opportunities as men:

Que si les dames arrivent moins souvent que les hommes, aux degrez d'excellence, c'est merveille que le deffaut de bonne instruction, voire l'affluence de la mauvaise expresse et professoire ne face pis, les gardant d'y pouvoir arriver du tout.

p. 65

(If women achieve levels of excellence less often than men, it is a wonder that the lack of a good education, indeed the proliferation of bad teaching, does not make it worse, preventing them from achieving any level at all.)

Later in the century, education was to become an important point of debate in Mlle de Scudéry's salon. Moreover, the tensions which existed between a woman entering society and the lack of attention paid to furthering her mind are displayed strongly in Mlle de Scudéry's *Le grand Cyrus*, where the character Sapho proclaims:

Y a-t-il rien de plus bizarre, que de voir comment on agit pour l'ordinaire, en l'éducation des Femmes? On ne veut point qu'elles soient coquettes, ni galantes; et on leur permet pourtant d'apprendre soigneusement, tout ce qui est propre à la galanterie, sans leur

permettre de savoir rien qui puisse fortifier leur vertu, ni occuper
leur esprit.

livre, X

(Is there anything more strange than to behold how women's
education is usually handled? Women are not supposed to be either
flirtatious or refined, and yet they are allowed to study copiously
everything to do with refinement without being allowed to know
anything about how to strengthen their virtue or occupy their
minds.)

Amongst other books of note (all written, paradoxically, by men)
which acknowledged the need for women to attain greater autonomy are Georges de Scudéry's *Femmes illustres* (1642), Jacques Du
Bosc's *Femme héroïque* (1645), Pierre Le Moyne's *Galerie des femmes
fortes* (1647), and, perhaps most significantly, various feminist tracts
written between 1673 and 1675 by François Poulain de la Barre.
Poulain de la Barre was a disciple of Descartes, and for the first
time rationalism was used as the basis for offering coherent arguments in favour of equality between the sexes.

2. Cross-Over

As surprisingly modern as these attitudes towards women may
seem in the carefully regulated age of Louis XIII and Louis XIV,
it is possibly more astonishing to find that alternative forms of
sexuality were both practised and written about. The abbé de
Choisy (1644-1724), for example, was known for his conquest of
numerous ladies, as one would expect with any self-respecting
clergyman of the time. However, he also enjoyed dressing up in
women's clothes, which is perhaps less probable. So convincing
was he that he used to entertain bishops and noblemen, posing
variously as Mme de Sancy and the comtesse des Barres, without
their guessing either his real identity or his gender. His memoirs,
entitled *Mémoires de l'abbé de Choisy habillé en femme* (Memoirs of the

abbé de Choisy dressed as a woman) were published posthumously.

An interesting progression takes place in the course of the memoir entitled *Histoire de Madame la comtesse des Barres*. Initially, even when his cross-dressing has begun and he is perceived by others as a woman, Choisy writes himself in the masculine gender. Only later does he begin to write himself in the feminine, as for example when he mentions that 'j'allais ainsi parée et ajustée à la grand'messe de ma paroisse' (I went to High Mass in my parish dressed and changed in this way) (p. 109). He delights also in the theatricality of his disguise, going so far as to act a scene from Corneille's *Polyeucte*, where he, accepted by others as the comtesse des Barres, plays the female role of Pauline and his young female charge, Mademoiselle de la Grise, plays the male role of Sévère. The transgression of sexual boundaries is further emphasized when the young Roselie is made by the 'comtesse' to dress as a boy:

> C'était un fort joli cavalier, et il me semblait que je l'en aimais davantage; je l'appelais mon petit mari; on l'appelait partout le petit comte ou M. comtin; il me servait d'écuyer. Je me lassai de lui voir une perruque, et lui fit couper un peu de cheveux; elle avait une tête charmante, ce qui la rendait bien plus jolie; la perruque vieillit les jeunes gens.
>
> p. 72

> (He was a very pretty horseman, and it seemed that I loved him more for it; I called him my little husband, and everywhere he was called the little Count or M. Comtin; he acted as my equerry. I did not want to see her wearing a wig, and so had her hair cut a little; her head was captivating, which made her even prettier; wigs age young people.)

Although another form of heterosexuality is imposed by the woman dressed as a man posing as the husband of a man dressed as a woman, the homoerotic subtext of the man finding the boyish charms of the girl attractive cannot be ignored.

I have chosen to mention this particular example not only

because of the bizarre novelty of the story but because of the ways this tale both does and does not conform to the age. First, if we consider the stereotype of the seventeenth century as inflexible and carefully controlled, obviously the abbé de Choisy cannot be seen as typical. Yet, paradoxically, he needs the rules to be in place in order for him to experience fully the sense of transgression of those rules. This is not unlike the point I have made in earlier chapters about the restrictions within which writers of the time operated. The tensions which are generated by the working against or within regulations, be they literary or moral, are largely what gives the seventeenth century its dynamism and flexibility. Another aspect of the abbé de Choisy story is completely typical of much literature from the time: the ludic nature of texts. Choisy's game of disguising himself within real life symbolizes the importance of performance, artifice and game-playing in literature of the time. This is evident in genres as diverse as comedy (where often disguise plays an important part), Pascal's Wager (fragment 418 of the *Pensées*), where the reader is enjoined to take part in a game, the maxim, which requires the reader to decode the concision of the form, the enigma, where a riddle must be solved, and the portrait, which often requires the reader or listener to guess the identity of the person being described.

The theatre provides a more likely scenario for cross-dressing. However, as can be seen in Chappuzeau's cautiously chosen words in *Le Théâtre français* (1674), he recognizes the difficulties of embracing too enthusiastically a practice which was outlawed in society at large:

> Je ne sais s'il est moins blâmable de voir des hommes travestis en femmes et prendre l'habit d'un autre sexe que le leur, ce qui hors de pareilles occasions, et des temps accordés aux réjouissances publiques, est punissable et défendu par les lois.
>
> *Le Théâtre français*, 1674, *Livre* I

> (I do not know if it is any less blameworthy to see men dressed as women and putting on clothes of the other sex, which, apart from

on such occasions and at certain times given over to public celebration, is punishable and prohibited by the laws of the land.)

Unlike with Shakespeare in England where women's roles were played by boys, in seventeenth-century France mostly women played the female roles. The plays where men play women and vice versa are therefore significant. To take the example of Molière, we encounter different kinds of cross-dressing. In *Le Dépit amoureux*, the central female character, Dorothée, disguises herself as a man, Ascagne, and then indulges in amorous talk with another man, Valère. Valère is so struck upon seeing 'him' on a subsequent occasion that he utters the words:

> La surprise me flatte, et je me sens saisir
> De merveille à la fois, d'amour et de plaisir.
>
> V, 8, 1759-60

(The surprise touches me, and I feel enraptured with love and pleasure at the same time)

Although Dorothée's identity is eventually revealed, the scenes where Valère finds himself drawn to his supposedly male friend do not exclude a homosexual reading.

Another kind of cross-dressing in Molière centres on a female character played throughout by a man, without any hint of disguise. A number of female characters were first played by men in Molière's own production of his plays, such as Philaminte in *Les Femmes savantes*, Mme Jourdain in *Le Bourgeois gentilhomme* and Mme Pernelle in *Tartuffe*. If we take the last example, the choice to have Mme Pernelle played by a man has both comic and serious implications. On the one level, her absurdity is accentuated by the incongruity of a man playing the matriarch (like a pantomime dame). On the other level, the theme of blind patriarchy (epitomized by Orgon and Mme Pernelle's obsession with Tartuffe) threatening the mainly female household is further enhanced by having Mme Pernelle played by a man.

The theme of transvestism evidently is accompanied by the idea of disguise and the blurring of sexual identity. An untitled sonnet by the *libertin* writer Saint-Pavin (1595-1670) exploits both these notions:

Caliste, propre et bien frisée,
Forçant l'ordre de son destin,
Pour me venir voir, un matin,
S'était en Page déguisée.

La petite, assez avisée,
Craignait qu'en jupe de satin,
A son teint délicat et fin
La porte lui fût refusée.

A l'aspect de ses doux appas,
J'arcai, je ne m'en défends pas,
Mais elle parut si gentille

Que pour la sauver du soupçon
Je la traitai comme une fille
Qui voulait passer pour garçon.

(Caliste, clean and curly-haired, trying to change her destiny, had disguised herself as a page one morning, in order to come and visit me. Ever alert, the little girl feared that the door would not be opened to her with her delicate complexion and if she wore a satin skirt. On seeing her sweet appearance, I will not deny that I was taken aback, but she appeared so lovely that in order to save her from suspicion, I treated her like a girl who wanted to be taken for a boy.)

The sonnet-form implies historically a love poem but this poem, through its obfuscation of sexual boundaries, deliberately subverts this traditional notion of love and explores the related question of sexual identity.

Homosexuality

Judging from the carefully sanitized editions and discussions of seventeenth-century *libertin* (free-thinking) poetry in this and previous centuries, one could be justified in thinking that either homosexuality did not exist in the seventeenth century or at least that gay writers decided to give the morally upright century a miss. One of the twentieth century's foremost scholars of the seventeenth century, Antoine Adam, omits Saint-Pavin from his volume of *libertin* poetry, mentioning elsewhere that Saint-Pavin's poems depict 'les vices contre nature' (vices against nature) and, moreover, are full of 'immondes grossièretés' (revolting coarseness). It should be stressed that in the seventeenth century there was no such notion as a 'gay identity'. However, a number of other *libertin* poets, in addition to their celebration of Epicurean ideals (the pursuit of pleasure) and their non-conformity in matters of religion, wrote poems on a homosexual theme. The most prominent of these was Saint-Pavin's friend and mentor, Théophile de Viau, whose popularity as a poet is shown by the 93 editions of his poetry which were published in the course of the seventeenth century. Others include Des Barreaux and Boisrobert, one of the founding members of the Académie française. The presence of homosexuality was not limited to an undercover group. The King's own brother, Philippe d'Orléans, was widely known for his homosexual liaisons (referred to by, amongst others, Tallemant des Réaux and Mme de Sévigné). One of Saint-Pavin's poems, 'Sur Louis XIV et Monsieur', refers explicitly to the homosexuality of Philippe d'Orléans, playing particularly on not specifying which of the two brothers is most shameful of his exploits:

Amour de diverses façons
Brûla deux frères de ses flammes,
L'un a soupiré pour les dames,
L'autre n'aima que les garçons.
S'il est vrai qu'un d'eux se retire,
De son péché las et honteux,

Il n'est pas malaisé de dire
Lequel ce doit être des deux.

(Two brothers burned with the flames of love in different ways; one
sighed for women and the other loved only boys. If it is true that
one of them is withdrawing from his sad and shameful sin, it is not
difficult to say which of the two it must be.)

Another untitled poem appears at first to be a conventional love
sonnet (where in the first twelve lines the gender of the loved one
is kept ambiguous), but in the final two lines we realize that it is in
fact addressed to Louis XIV himself:

Amour, vis-tu jamais un si parfait ouvrage?
Que ces beaux jours sont doux, que leurs traits sont perçants;
Et qu'il est malaisé d'empêcher que mes sens
Ne soumettent mon âme aux lois de son servage.

Jamais une Beauté ne piqua davantage.
Elle me plaît en tout; et ses charmes puissants
Sont plus à redouter, plus ils sont innocents;
Et moins elle y consent, et plus elle m'engage.

Sa grâce et son esprit ensemble également
Partagent le pouvoir d'acquérir un Amant;
Ses rares qualités la rendent sans seconde.

Et pour dire quelle est cette merveille, Amour;
Elle porte le nom du plus grand Roi du monde,
Joint à celui qu'au Ciel il aura quelque jour.

(Love, did you ever see such a perfect work of art? How sweet these
beautiful days are and how piercing are their characteristics; it is
difficult to prevent my senses from submitting my soul to the laws
of service to this love. Never has a beauty been so striking. It pleases
me in all things, and its powerful charms are even more to be feared
the more they are innocent; and the less this beauty gives way the
more it engages my attention. Its grace and spirit together share the

same power as acquiring a lover. Its rare qualities make it unparalleled. And to say what this marvel is, O Love; it carries the name of the greatest King in the world, joined to the King in heaven whom he will meet one day.)

This sonnet could be interpreted as a satire on the traditional poem of praise to the monarch, where at the same time the poet subverts the norms of heterosexual love poetry. It could also be seen in its subversion as a poem written by someone free of the hierarchical structures of the court, but this would be an erroneous assumption. Saint-Pavin himself was close to those in power and in 1666 was named honorary chaplain and counsellor to Louis XIV. Moreover, contemporary reports show that he was regarded as epitomizing the best qualities of *honnêteté*. He frequented the salons, and Méré (whose discussion of *honnêteté* was considered in Chapter 5) even sent him the manuscript of one of his works, *De la justesse*, for approval. As he was so closely linked to the salons, it is not surprising to see that he joined in the common practice of writing a self-portrait. In keeping with the Epicurean doctrine of pursuing pleasure, he deliberately blurs the distinction between vice and virtue:

Et jusqu'ici je n'ai point su
Ce que c'est que vice ou vertu.

(Up to now, I have never known what vice or virtue is.)

However, more than simply following fashionable doctrines, Saint-Pavin throws into question many givens by exploring the realms of conventional morality. In her article on Saint-Pavin, listed in the bibliography at the end of this chapter, Kathleen Collins makes the useful point that Saint-Pavin's libertine philosophy and his association with many *honnêtes gens* of the day are not necessarily incompatible, that 'this absorption of two value systems results in a more complex stance than the mere donning of a disguise' (p. 175). I would go further: Saint-Pavin embodies many tensions of the age.

On several levels, codes of politeness and civilized living coexist with the questioning of the rules and norms which define that society.

We have seen throughout this book the recurring motif of the reliance on ancient classical sources. Théophile's and later Saint-Pavin's homosexual verse is no exception. Both write poems on the model of homosexual verse by Latin writers such as Martial and Virgil. The reference to these sources shows both the continuing use of intertextuality (frequent allusion to, and imitation of other texts) in all seventeenth-century genres and (of greater urgency to the poets) the need to give their poetry a legitimacy which was threatened by charges of obscenity.

Théophile was imprisoned on the interrelated charges of free-thought and sodomy. A poem, 'A un Sien Ami', written while he was in prison, is believed to be addressed to his former lover Des Barreaux, who renounced him at the time of his imprisonment. It is remarkable for its unequivocal declaration of love for another man, despite the sense of betrayal which permeates the poem:

> L'excès de mon malheur n'est cruel qu'en ce point
> Qui me dit, malgré moi, que tu ne m'aimes point …
> Je t'eusse fait jadis passer les Pyrénées,
> J'eusse attaché tes jours avec mes années,
> Et conduit mes desseins au cours de mon destin
> Des bords de l'Occident jusqu'au flot du matin,
> Et je n'ai rien commis, même dans mon courage,
> Qui te puisse obliger à me tourner visage,
> Puisque je n'ai rien fait, et j'en jure les dieux,
> Que t'aimer, ô Tircis, tous les jours un peu mieux.

(My extreme unhappiness is cruel only because it tells me that, in spite of myself, you do not love me at all … In the past I would have crossed the Pyrenees for you, I would have joined your days with my years, followed my projects as destiny led me from the edges of the West to where morning breaks, and I have done nothing, even at my most courageous times, which might oblige you to turn your

face from me, since I have done nothing other (and I swear this by
the gods) than to love you only a little more every day .)

In the theatre, where the need to respect the *bienséances* was all-important, not surprisingly there are very few direct references to
homosexual love. However, it is worth mentioning the two playwrights whom I referred to at the very beginning, Racine and
Corneille. In Racine's *Bérénice*, it is hinted that the bond between
Titus and Antiochus might have been closer than mere friendship
(lines 100, 113, 270, 672, 1435-6). Although it is in no way explicit
and does not undermine the love which both Titus and Antiochus
feel for Bérénice, this reading gives added significance to the role
of Antiochus, who otherwise seems greatly diminished when compared to Titus and Bérénice, and to the triangular passion of the
three protagonists. In Corneille's early play *Clitandre* (1632), the
relationship between the prince Floridan and his favourite Clitandre is more explicit. Clitandre is referred to by Corneille in his
Argument at the head of the play as the Prince's 'mignon', and
throughout the play the prince reiterates his love for Clitandre.
The most specific example of physical closeness, unusual in any
manifestation in seventeenth-century theatre, occurs through the
Prince's words in:

A l'ombre des ormeaux l'un dans l'autre enlacés
Clitandre m'entretient de ses travaux passés.

II, 4, 535-6

(In the shade of the elm trees, entwined with each other, Clitandre
tells me of his past exploits.)

Although it could be the elms which are inter-laced (the masculine
plural past participle renders this line ambiguous), given the love of
the two men for each other, it seems probable that it is they who
are entwined.

Although the patriarchal society of the time inevitably made
both society and family male-dominated, on all levels we find

exceptions to the rules or the norms which governed them. But, far from being eccentric examples which should remain in the margins of any consideration of seventeenth-century France, they exemplify the tensions which are so central to the age.

Selected Reading

Antoine Adam, *Les Libertins au XVIIe siècle* (Paris, 1964). Very good information on the *libertin* poets, but, as mentioned in this chapter, little attention is paid to homosexual verse. In French.

Kathleen Collins, 'Pleasure's Artful Garb: poetic strategies of Denis Sanguin de Saint-Pavin (1595-1670)', in *Continuum* 3 (1991), pp. 171-89. A significant piece of scholarship on an unjustly neglected poet.

Elizabeth Guild, ' "Le moyen de faire de cela un grand homme": the abbé de Choisy and the unauthorized body of representation', *Romantic Review* vol. 85 no. 2 (March 1994) 179-190. A stimulating study of cross-dressing in the abbé de Choisy's Memoirs.

Michael Hawcroft, 'Homosexual love in Corneille's *Clitandre* (1632)', in *Seventeenth-Century French Studies* XV (1993), pp. 135-144. A thorough and insightful reading of this early play by Pierre Corneille.

Maurice Lever, *Les Bûchers de Sodome* (Paris, 1985). A wide-ranging survey of homosexuality, with a section devoted to the seventeenth century. Somewhat superficial but a useful introduction. In French.

Ian Maclean, *Woman Triumphant: feminism in French literature 1610-1652* (Oxford, 1977). A very important work on women writers and the perception of women in seventeenth-century France.

Richard Parish, 'Molière en Travesti: transvestite acting in Molière', in *Nottingham French Studies* vol. 33, no. 1 (Spring 1994), pp. 53-8. An interesting discussion of a surprisingly neglected dimension of Molière's theatre.

8

Conclusions

Rather than offering a simple summary of the concerns of this book, I have chosen in this conclusion to focus on one writer whom I have mentioned several times already, whose life spans much of the seventeenth century and who encapsulates in her writings many of the tensions which have been explored in previous chapters: Madame de Sévigné (1626-1696). Because her letters cannot be placed into any single formal category, the wide-ranging subject matter of her discussions transcends narrow boundaries and provides a useful starting point for an overview of the tensions of seventeenth-century French writing.

As a woman writer (channeling her undoubted creative energies in her letters) and frequenter of the salons, she epitomizes the intellectually independent woman of those circles. She was a friend of Mme de Lafayette and Mlle de Scudéry, taking great interest in genres as diverse as novels (where she comments both on Mlle de Scudéry's novels and the appearance of *La Princesse de Clèves*), the theatre, poetry, sermons and portraits. Her unorthodox education (unlike most women she was given a wide-ranging education, taught mostly by her uncle, the abbé de Coulanges) made her widely read in and comfortable with Latin and Italian. Her references to ancient and contemporary literature make her letters rich with the kind of intertextuality which nourishes so much literature of the century. The subject-matter of her letters range from daily gossip to considerations of the after-life.

In many ways, her intellectual autonomy resulted from the very constraints which circumscribed many women of her position. Her husband, who had been involved in numerous affairs, was killed in a duel over one of his mistresses. Mme de Sévigné therefore found herself widowed at the age of 25. In her correspondence (consisting of some 1400 letters), she mentions her husband very seldom, but the occasional glimpse of the pain caused by him shows only too forcefully her awareness of the unjustness of her husband's actions. Paradoxically, his death gave her a freedom which many married women could not have. In a letter written to her cousin after the death of her beloved uncle, the abbé de Coulanges, she displays not only her gratitude to her uncle and the lingering pain over her husband's actions many years before, but also her recognition of the subsequent growth of her personal and intellectual character:

> Je reprends dès les derniers jours de la vie de mon cher oncle l'Abbé [Coulanges], à qui, comme vous savez, j'avais des obligations infinies. Je lui devais la douceur et le repos de ma vie; c'est à lui à qui vous devez la joie que j'apportais dans votre société. Sans lui, nous n'aurions jamais ri ensemble; vous lui devez toute ma gaieté, ma belle humeur, ma vivacité, le don que j'avais de vous bien entendre, l'intelligence qui me faisait comprendre ce que vous aviez dit et deviner ce que vous alliez dire; en un mot, le bon Abbé, en me retirant des abîmes où M. de Sévigné m'avait laissée, m'a rendue telle que j'étais, telle que vous m'avez vue, et digne de votre estime et de votre amitié.

> To Bussy-Rabutin, 13 November 1687

(I take up my story from the last days of my dear uncle the Abbé, to whom, as you know, I was infinitely obliged. I owed him the sweetness and restfulness of my life, and it is to him that you owe the joy that I brought to your society. Without him, never would we have laughed together. You owe him all my gaiety, good humour and vivacity, the gift I had of understanding you, the intelligence which made me grasp what you had said and guess what you were going to say. In a word, the good Abbé, pulling me from the abyss where M de Sévigné had left me, has made me what I was, as you have seen me, worthy of both your respect and your friendship.)

Quite apart from her deference to her uncle, we see how Mme de Sévigné depicts herself as the intellectual equal of her male cousin. The repetition of the verb 'devoir' shows how both Mme de Sévigné and Bussy-Rabutin are indebted to Coulanges for her abilities, which were nurtured after the death of her husband. It is interesting to note also the verbs depicting these abilities: 'entendre', 'comprendre', 'deviner'. Although she displayed great social capabilities, she saw herself as having the gifts of listening, understanding and anticipating the meaning of others. This idea of participation is vital to our comprehension of the many levels of reading seventeenth-century texts. In the theatre, for example, aspects like the presence of non-speaking characters, the subtext and the spectators are often as important as the lines being spoken. Similarly, in reading seventeenth-century texts, our awareness of the very process of and different levels of reading can be as central as the subject-matter of those works.

Another result of the loss of her husband was that Mme de Sévigné devoted her attention to her daughter, the Comtesse de Grignan, who was based in Provence. In her letters to her daughter, she employs the passions and energies which one might expect of a lover, thereby redefining the traditional parameters of a love letter. Moreover, despite the attempts of a number of men, she made the decision not to remarry, and her reiteration of her autonomy and her expressions of horror at her daughter's frequent pregnancies, while not matching the commitment of feminist writings of the time, show a determination not to subscribe to the prevalent patriarchal expectations.

In the first four chapters, I discussed the political tensions which permeated the theatre and the Church, in addition to the sense of conflict which existed both within the rules and in working against the rules. In her letters, Mme de Sévigné is often a first-hand witness of those conflicts. She reports, for example, her reaction to new plays by Racine and Corneille; she talks about her enjoyment of the *Lettres provinciales* and discusses the conflict between the Jansenists and Jesuits. While she and many of her friends were sympathetic towards Port-Royal, she also expresses her admiration for Jesuit preachers, such as Bourdaloue. Moreover, she was personally involved in one of the major political controversies of the 1660s.

Her friend, Nicolas Fouquet, Surintendant des Finances under Louis XIV, was arrested and tried in 1664-5 for fraud and treason. It is thought that jealous rivals, most notably Colbert, had masterminded the arrest. The trial gripped the whole of Paris. As the charge of treason carried with it the death penalty, Fouquet's supporters were justifiably concerned. Mme de Sévigné wrote a series of reports to another friend of Fouquet, Pomponne. In the final analysis, Fouquet was found guilty of financial malpractice but not guilty of treason. Although he was spared the death sentence, he was first banished and then put in prison on the orders of Louis XIV. Supporters of Fouquet themselves needed to be circumspect in case they incurred the wrath of the King. One letter in particular exemplifies many of the tensions of this event:

Il faut que je vous conte ce que j'ai fait. Imaginez-vous que des dames m'ont proposé d'aller dans une maison qui regarde droit dans l'Arsenal, pour voir revenir notre pauvre ami [Fouquet]. J'étais masquée, je l'ai vu venir d'assez loin. M. d'Artagnan était auprès de lui; cinquante mousquetaires derrière, à trente ou quarante pas. Il paraissait assez rêveur. Pour moi, quand je l'ai aperçu, les jambes m'ont tremblé, et le coeur m'a battu si fort, que je n'en pouvais plus. En s'approchant de nous pour rentrer dans son trou, M. d'Artagnan l'a poussé, et lui a fait remarquer que nous étions là. Il nous a donc saluées, et a pris cette mine riante que vous connaissez. Je ne crois pas qu'il m'ait reconnue; mais je vous avoue que j'ai été étrangement saisi, quand je l'ai vu rentrer dans cette petite porte. Si vous saviez combien on est malheureuse quand on a le coeur fait comme je l'ai, je suis assurée que vous auriez pitié de moi; mais je pense que vous n'en êtes pas quitte à meilleur marché, de la manière dont je vous connais.

To M. de Pomponne, 27 November 1664

(I must tell you what I did. Imagine it: some women suggested that

I go into a house which looks directly onto the Arsenal, to see our poor friend return. I was masked, and could see him coming from quite a distance. M d'Artagnan was next to him, and there were fifty musketeers about thirty or forty paces behind him. He seemed quite lost in his thoughts. As for me, when I noticed him, my legs started trembling and my heart beat so loudly that it was almost unbearable. As he came towards us to re-enter his little cell, M d'Artagnan nudged him and let him know that we were there. He then waved to us and took on that laughing expression which you know so well. I do not think he recognized me, but I must confess that I was strangely moved to see him go through that little door. If only you knew how unhappy you are if you have a heart like mine, I am sure that you would have pity on me; but I do not think you would be any less moved, knowing you as I do.)

The interplay of differing tensions gives the letter a complexity which goes beyond the mere details of a particular event. On one level, it is necessary for Mme de Sévigné to remain disguised: because of the immediate threat of being discovered as sympathetic to Fouquet, her role as spectator is fraught with danger. On another level, she is showing the reduced circumstances of their friend Fouquet (exemplified in such words as 'trou' and 'petite porte') and the danger to him (incarnated by 'cinquante mousquetaires'). They are both constricted and yet they both contravene the powers by their brief interaction. Two narratives coexist in this letter: the description of Fouquet's return to prison and the description of Mme de Sévigné's reactions to his arrest. Yet even in these two narratives, there are further complexities. Mme de Sévigné is describing their friend's courage to Pomponne, evoking pity for Fouquet's plight. But she is also evoking pity from her correspondent for her own despair at the sight of Fouquet. Quite apart from Fouquet's presence, there is a completely different level of interaction in the letter. Mme de Sévigné is establishing a level of intimacy between herself and Pomponne, first by anticipating his sympathy for her distress ('vous auriez pitié de moi') and second by recognizing his (Pomponne's) own sensibilities ('la manière dont je vous connais'). The terminology is precisely that of the effect of tragedy. It shows Mme de Sévigné's sense of theatricality, but conversely, it shows how real the tragic emotions were for spectators in the theatre at the time. The formulas used to evoke tragic emotion are not simply artificial constructs.

Another tragic emotion, fear, is evoked in a letter from Mme de Sévigné to her daughter, where she speaks of the uncertainty of death. Although she was a practising Christian, she still was not afraid to question her faith and her motivations. Again, such attitudes are integral to the age in which she lived. Although on the surface, we find, especially in the later years of the century, the crushing of religious resistance, underneath there existed much greater scepticism and questioning:

> Vous me demandez, ma chère enfant, si j'aime toujours bien la vie. Je vous avoue que j'y trouve des chagrins cuisants; mais je suis encore plus dégoûtée de la mort: je me trouve si malheureuse d'avoir à finir tout ceci par elle, que si je pouvais retourner en arrière, je ne demanderais pas mieux. Je me trouve dans un engagement qui m'embarrasse: je suis embarquée dans la vie sans mon consentement; il faut que j'en sorte, cela m'assomme; et comment en sortirai-je? Par où? Par quelle porte? Quand sera-ce? En quelle disposition? Souffrirai-je mille et mille douleurs, qui me feront mourir désespérée? Aurai-je un transport au cerveau? Mourrai-je d'un accident? Comment serai-je avec Dieu? Qu'aurai-je à lui présenter? La crainte, la nécessité, feront-elles mon retour vers lui? N'aurai-je aucun autre sentiment que celui de la peur? Que puis-je espérer? Suis-je digne du paradis? Suis-je digne de l'enfer? Quelle alternative! Quel embarras! Rien n'est si fou que de mettre son salut dans l'incertitude; mais rien n'est si naturel, et la sotte vie que je mène est la chose du monde la plus aisée à comprendre.
>
> To her daughter, 16 March 1672

(You ask me, my dear child, if I still love life. I admit that I have a number of terrible worries, but I am even more disgusted by death; I become so unhappy to have to finish everything with death that if I could go back in time I would ask for nothing better. I find myself pushed along in a way which concerns me; I am launched upon life without my consent, a life which I must leave, and that overwhelms me. How will I leave life? Where? Through which door? When will that be? What will my disposition be? Will I suffer from thousands of pains which will make me die in a state of despair? Will I have a seizure of the brain? Will I die from an accident? How will I be with God? What will I have to present to him? Will fear and necessity make me return to him? Will I have any feeling other than fear? What am I to hope for? Am I worthy to be in paradise? Am I worthy to be in Hell? What an alternative! What a terrible situation! Nothing seems so mad as to place one's salvation in a state of uncertainty; but nothing is so natural, and the stupid life that I lead is the easiest thing in the world to comprehend.)

Another stereotype of the seventeenth century is that of complete order and constraint. By exploring genres such as the fragment I hope to have shown that disorder is as powerful a driving force as order. Mme de Sévigné herself voices this fascination ('admirer') with the changeability and disorder of the world:

> N'admirez-vous point comme tout est mêlé en ce monde, et comme rien n'est pur, ni longtemps dans une même disposition?
> To her daughter, 24 November 1679

> (Do you not wonder at how everything is mingled in this world and how nothing is pure or in the same disposition for long?)

A major point which I have made throughout this book is the positive creative force of the tensions which underpin so many writings of the seventeenth century: for example, many of Molière's plays result directly from the conflicts of the day; also, Pascal's *Lettres provinciales* emanate from the religious controversies. But also I hope to have shown that the different genres are themselves governed by more complex factors. In the theatre, for instance, playwrights like Corneille and Racine and theorists like D'Aubignac recognized the importance of spectator reaction. Similarly, many writers, such as Pascal and La Bruyère, anticipate reader reaction as fundamental to the creative process. A similar point seems to be recognized by Mme de Sévigné in the way that her correspondent reshapes the original letter:

> C'est entre vos mains, ma chère enfant, que mes lettres deviennent de l'or: quand elles sortent des miennes, je les trouve si grosses et si pleines de paroles, que je dis: 'Ma fille n'aura pas le temps de lire tout cela.'
>
> To her daughter, 8 January 1690

> (It is in your hands, my dear child, that my letters become gold. When they leave mine, I find them so clumsy and packed with words that I say: 'My daughter will not have the time to read all that.')

The writings from the seventeenth century may to some extent be bound by *bienséances* and regulations, but they are not set in stone. Their very vitality comes from interaction on many levels. And that is where we as present readers fit in. Our reading, our interpretation of the texts form as integral a part of the creative process as they were in the seventeenth century. Although, as we have seen, the writings are very much of their time, reflecting the tastes and fashions of a privileged society, often the writings display a self-mocking awareness of the absurdity of their age which transcends any limitations.

Perhaps in future, rather than taking the rules alone as the focus of the seventeenth century, we can recognize that it is the coexistence of rules and tensions in all their manifestations both on and below the surface which are the true driving force of French writings from the time. In our reading of the texts, the rules may on one level be imprisoning, but it is the tensions generated by those constraints which are ultimately liberating.

Selected Reading

R. Duchêne, *Naissances d'un écrivain: Madame de Sévigné* (Paris, 1996). One of many books on Mme de Sévigné by Duchêne. This is useful on her techniques as a writer.

M. Hawcroft, 'Historical Evidence and Literature: Madame de Sévigné's letters on the trial of Fouquet', *The Seventeenth Century* vol. IX no. 1 (Spring 1994), pp. 57-75. A subtle analysis of the Fouquet trial.

Glossary of Seventeenth-Century French Literary Figures

Ailly, abbé d' (dates unknown): maxim-writer and churchman, author of *Pensées diverses* (1678).

Annat, François (1590-1670): Jesuit and implacable opponent of the Jansenists.

Arnauld, Angélique (1591-1661): abbess at Port-Royal, sister of Antoine.

Arnauld, Antoine (1612-94): leading theologian at Port-Royal, author of many works, including the influential *Grammaire générale et raisonnée* (1660, with Lancelot) and *La Logique, ou l'Art de penser* (1662, with Nicole).

Arnauld d'Andilly, Robert (1588-1674): translator, most notably of St Augustine.

Assoucy, Charles Coypeau d' (1605-77): author of burlesque songs.

Aubignac, abbé d' (1604-76): critic and dramatic theorist, author of *La Pratique du théâtre* (1657) and *Dissertations contre Corneille* (1663).

Aulnoy, Marie-Catherine le Jumel de Barneville, comtesse d' (*c.* 1650-1705): author, best known for her fairy-tales.

Baillet, Adrien (1649-1706): Jansenist priest and bibliographer.

Balzac, Guez de (1594-1654): prose writer and critic, known especially for imposing order and regularity on prose, in imitation of antiquity; author of *Lettres* (published regularly from 1624), *Le Prince* (1631), *Socrate chrétien* and *Entretiens* (published posthumously in 1657).

Barbier d'Aucour, Jean (1641-94): Jansenist polemicist.

Barbin, Claude (1629-1700): bookseller and publisher.

Barcos, Martin de (1600-78): theologian at Port-Royal; successor to his uncle Jean Duvergier de Hauranne as abbé de Saint-Cyran.

Bary, René (1640-80): author of *La Rhétorique française* (1653).

Bayle, Pierre (1647-1706): best known for his *Dictionnaire historique et critique* (1697 and 1702), spokesman for religious toleration.

Bellegarde, Jean-Baptiste Morvan de (1648-1734): author on civility, religion and ethics.

Benserade, Isaac de (1613-91): poet and dramatist, author of libretti for court ballets with the composer Lully in the 1660s.

Bernard, Catherine (*c.* 1662-1712): author and playwright.

Béroalde de Verville (1556-*c.* 1629): author of diverse works, best known for *Le Moyen de parvenir* (1610).

Bérulle, Pierre de (1575-1629): cardinal and religious reformer, founder in 1611 of the Oratory.

Boileau, known as Despréaux, Nicolas (1636-1711): poet, satirist and critic, author of *L'Art poétique* (1674), the mock-heroic *Le Lutrin* and numerous *Epîtres* and *Satires*. Vigorous defender of the *anciens* in the *Querelle des anciens et des modernes*.

Boisrobert, François le Métel (1589-1662): poet, novelist and dramatist, founding member of the Académie française.

Bossuet, Jacques-Bénigne (1627-1704): bishop of Meaux, prominent preacher and historian, known especially for his published funeral orations.

Boucher, Jean (1560-1631): priest and preacher.

Bouhours, Dominique (1628-1702): Jesuit critic and grammarian.

Bourdaloue, Louis (1623-1704): popular Jesuit preacher, praised amongst others by Mme de Sévigné.

Brantôme, Pierre de Bourdeilles, seigneur de (*c.* 1540-1614): memorialist, whose various *Vies* were published posthumously.

Bussy-Rabutin, Roger, comte de (1618-93); soldier and author; cousin of Mme de Sévigné; best known for his scandalous court chronicle, *Histoire amoureuse des Gaules* (1665), which resulted in his imprisonment and exile.

Camus, Jean-Pierre (*c.* 1584-1652): bishop of Belley, writer of *Diversités* (1609-1618) and *Esprit du B. François de Sales* (1639-41), one of the first French bishops to espouse the ideals of the Council of Trent.

Champaigne, Philippe de (1602-74): painter of religious portraits, associated with Port-Royal.

Chapelain, Jean (1595-1674): theorist and critic, founding member of the Académie française, author of the Académie's consideration of Pierre Corneille's *Le Cid* and of the much criticized epic *La Pucelle* (1656).

Chappuzeau, Samuel (1625-1701): author of *Le Théâtre français* (1674).

Charpentier, Marc-Antoine (*c.* 1645-1704): composer, including the incidental music for Molière's *Le Malade imaginaire*.

Charron, Pierre (1541-1603): preacher and moral philosopher, author of *Les Trois Vérités* (1593) and *De la Sagesse* (1601), both of which were very influential in seventeenth-century France.

Choisy, abbé de (1644-1724): cross-dressing priest and historian, author of *Journal du voyage de Siam* (1687) and two memoirs, *Histoire de Madame la comtesse des Barres* (published 1735) and *Histoire de Madame de Sancy* (published 1839).

Claude le Lorrain (1600-82): painter, particularly of landscapes.

Colbert, Jean-Baptiste (1619-83): chief minister of Louis XIV from 1661.

Colletet, Guillaume (1596-1659): poet and theorist, early member of the Académie française.

Condé, Louis de Bourbon, prince de (1621-86): influential patron of the arts.

Conrart, Valentin (1603-75): first secretary of the Académie française.

Conti, Armand, prince de (1629-68): participated in the Fronde, patron of Molière, author of *Traité de la comédie* (1666), which he wrote after turning to religion.

Corneille, Pierre (1606-84): dramatist and dramatic theorist, author of 32 plays, immensely popular in the seventeenth century. Best known for his tragedies *Le Cid* (1637), *Horace* (1640), *Cinna* (1641) and *Polyeucte* (1642), but also an accomplished comic dramatist, as shown in comedies like *L'Illusion comique* (1635) and *Le Menteur* (1644). In 1660, he published three *Discours* on dramatic theory and accompaning critical *Examens* to his plays.

Corneille, Thomas (1625-1709): younger brother of Pierre, author of over 30 plays and operas which did not attain the long-lasting success of his brother's plays.

Costar, Pierre (1603-60): wrote in defence of Voiture's poetry and was a friend of Guez de Balzac and Ménage.

Cotin, Charles (1604-82): preacher and poet, enemy of Boileau.

Coustel, Pierre (dates unknown): teacher at Port-Royal, author of treatises on education.

Cyrano de Bergerac (1619-55): soldier and writer, attached to *libertin* circles, renowned for his colourful life.

Des Barreaux, Jacques Vallée, sieur (1599-1673): *libertin*, occasional poet.

Descartes, René (1596-1650): enormously influential philosopher, known as father of modern philosophy and science, author of *Discours de la méthode* (1637), *Méditations* (1641), *Principes* (1644) and *Les Passions de l'âme* (1650).

Desmarets de Saint-Sorlin, Jean (1595-1676): dramatist and poet, author of many plays ordered by cardinal Richelieu, most notably the comedy *Les Visionnaires* (1638); first Chancellor of the Académie française.

Desportes, Philippe (1546-1606): poet, most popular in the seventeenth century for his translation of the Psalter.

Donneau de Visé, Jean (1638-1710): founder and editor of the periodical *Le Mercure galant*, author of a number of plays, and defender of Pierre Corneille in his dispute with D'Aubignac.

Du Bosc, Jacques (dates unknown): author of *L'Honnête Femme* (1632) and *La Femme héroïque* (1645).

Du Perron, Jacques (1556-1618): cardinal and poet.

Duplessis-Mornay, Philippe (1549-1623): leading Calvinist propagandist and supporter of Henri IV.

Du Ryer, Pierre (*c.* 1600-1658): dramatist and translator, author of 18 tragedies, comedies, tragi-comedies and pastorals.

Du Vair, Guillaume (1556-1621): Neostoic moralist and politician, immensely popular in the first half of the seventeenth century.

Esprit, Jacques (1611-78): author of *De la fausseté des vertus humaines* (1677-8), a strong condemnation of pagan virtues; also known as a conversationalist in the literary salons.

Faret, Nicolas (1596-1646): author of *L'Honnête Homme ou l'art de plaire à la cour* (1630), early member of the Académie française.

Fénelon, François de Salignac de la Mothe- (1651-1715): churchman, perhaps best known for the educational romance *Télémaque* (1693, published 1699), written for his charge the Duke of Burgundy (grandson of Louis XIV).

Ferrand, Anne de Bellinzani (1657-1740): writer of novels on unhappily married women, including *Histoire nouvelle des amours de la jeune Bélise et de Cléante* (1689) and the epistolary novel *Lettres galantes* (1691).

Filleau de la Chaise, Nicolas (1631-88): historian, critic and philosopher.

Fléchier, Esprit (1632-1710): orator and churchman, author of funeral orations which were often compared with those by Bossuet.

Fontenelle, Bernard Le Bovier de (1657-1757): member of the Académie française and at the end of the seventeenth century appointed Secrétaire Perpétuel of the Académie des sciences; on the side of the moderns in his *Digression sur les anciens et les modernes* (1688); author of the *Nouveaux dialogues des morts* (1683) and the *Entretiens sur la pluralité des mondes* (1686).

Foucquet or Fouquet, Nicolas (1615-80): chief finance minister of Louis XIV until his disgrace in 1661, reported by Mme de Sévigné; influential promoter of the arts.

François de Sales, Saint (1567-1622): founder in 1610 with St Jeanne-Françoise de Chantal of the Congregation of the Visitation; author of the influential manual on religious devotion, *Introduction à la vie dévote* (1609), and of *Traité de l'amour de Dieu* (1616).

Furetière, Antoine (1619-88): author of *Le Roman bourgeois* (1666); justly renowned for his *Dictionnaire universel* (1690), which rivalled the dictionary of the Académie française.

Galland, Antoine (1646-1715): translator and orientalist.

Garasse, François (1585-1631): Jesuit priest, fierce opponent of sceptics and *libertins*, author of *Doctrine curieuse des beaux-esprits de ce temps* (1623) and *Somme théologique* (1625).

Gassendi, Pierre (1592-1655): philosopher and priest; best known for his disputes with Descartes, his espousal of scepticism and his work on the philosopher Epicurus; author of the *Exercitationes* (1624).

Giry, Louis (1596-1666): translator.

Godeau, Antoine (1605-72): author of prose and verse, bishop of Grasse and then of Vence, known for his Jansenist sympathies, early member of the Académie française.

Gomberville, Marin le Roy, sieur de (1600-74): poet and author of prose, most notably *Polexandre* (1619-37), *Cythérée* (1639-40) and *La Jeune Alcidiane* (1651).

Goulard, Simon (1543-1628): scholar and translator.

Gournay, Marie le Jars, Mademoiselle de (*c.* 1566-1645): author of a number of works, most famously her *Egalité des hommes et des femmes* (1622); adopted daughter of Montaigne, entrusted with the final edition of his *Essais*.

Guilleragues, Gabriel-Joseph de Lavergne, vicomte de (1628-

85): lawyer and ambassador; assumed to be the author of the epistolary work, *Lettres portugaises* (1669).

Guyon, Jeanne-Marie Bouvier de la Motte (1648-1717): spiritual writer.

Habert de Montmort, Henri-Louis (*c.* 1600-79): founder of a scientific academy, which met at his home.

Hardy, Alexandre (*c.* 1572-1632): dramatist, author of 34 surviving tragedies, comedies and pastorals.

Hauteroche, Noël le Breton, sieur de (1617-1707): comic actor and playwright.

Huet, Pierre-Daniel (1630-1721): polymath, defender of modern literature, as shown in his *De l'origine des romans* (1670).

Jansenius, Cornelius (1585-1638): theologian, bishop of Ypres, author of the influential and controversial *Augustinus* (published posthumously 1640).

Jodelet (*c.* 1595-1660): actor, member of Molière's troupe from 1659.

La Bruyère, Jean de (1645-96): *moraliste*, author of *Les Caractères* (first edition 1688), an amalgam of writings of different lengths (maxims, portraits, essays) devoted to a study of mankind and society; known for his support of classical models in the *Querelle des anciens et des modernes*.

La Calprenède, Gauthier de Coste, sieur de (*c.* 1610-63): dramatist and author of historical romances; plays include *Le Comte d'Essex* (1637) and *La Mort des enfants d'Hérode* (1638).

La Fayette, Marie-Madeleine Pioche de La Vergne, comtesse de (1634-93): writer of prose fiction and historian, best known for *La Princesse de Clèves* (1678), which has been hailed as the first psychological novel; other fictional works include *La Princesse de Montpensier* (1662), *Zaïde* (1670) and *La Comtesse de Tende* (first published 1724).

La Fontaine, Jean de (1621-95): poet and fabulist, renowned for his *Fables* (first published 1668), drawn from such sources as Aesop and Phaedrus, but written in verse and constituting a commentary on his own age.

La Ménardière, Hippolyte-Jules Pilet de (1610-63): poet and doctor, remembered chiefly for his *Poétique* (1639), a theoretical work on the rules for tragedy.

La Mothe le Vayer, François de (1588-1672): proponent of scepticism, author of *Dialogues faits à l'imitation des anciens* (1630-1), *Hexaméron rustique* (1670) and the anti-Jansenist treatise *De la vertu des payens* (1642).

Lamy, Bernard (1640-1715): priest and author of the rhetorical treatise *La Rhétorique ou l'art de parler* (1675 and 1688).

Lancelot, Claude (1616-95): teacher and grammarian, author of several grammars for the Port-Royal schools and (together with Antoine Arnauld) of the important *Grammaire générale et raisonnée* (1660).

La Rochefoucauld, François, duc de (1613-80): *moraliste*, author of the hugely influential *Maximes* (1678), drawn from his experience of salon society and imbued with a resigned pessimism; he also played a prominent part in the Fronde as an ally of Condé against Mazarin; close friend of Mme de Lafayette.

La Sablière, Marguerite Hessein de (*c.* 1636-93): author of *Maximes chrétiennes*, but better known for her salon.

La Suze, Henriette de Coligny, comtesse de (1618-73): poet, admired for her elegies.

Le Clerc, Jean (1657-1736): scholar, author in the seventeenth century of his journals, *Bibliothèque universelle et historique* (1686-93).

Le Faucheur, Michel (*c.* 1585-1657): priest, author of *Traité de l'action de l'orateur ou de la prononciation et du geste* (1657).

Le Maistre, Antoine (1608-58): barrister and the first Jansenist *solitaire* at Port-Royal.

Le Maistre de Sacy, Louis-Isaac (1613-84): spiritual director, most notably of Pascal, and translator of the Port-Royal Bible (1667-96).

Le Moyne, Pierre (1602-71): Jesuit moralist and poet, author of *La Galerie des femmes fortes* (1647), focus of Pascal's satire in *Lettres provinciales*.

Lenclos, Ninon de (*c.* 1620-1705): celebrated courtesan and poet.

L'Héritier de Villandon, Marie-Jeanne (1664-1734): writer of fairy-tales, like her uncle Charles Perrault.

Lingendes, Jean (*c.* 1580-1616): poet.

Longueville, Anne-Geneviève de Bourbon-Condé (1619-79): salon personality, leader in the Fronde insurrection; latterly attached to the Carmelites and Jansenists.

Louis XIII (1601-43): King, whose chief minister was Richelieu; promoter of the arts.

Louis XIV (1638-1715): King, towering figure in the seventeenth century; patron of the arts.

Lully, Jean-Baptiste (1632-87): composer, regarded as founder of French opera, known initially for his *ballets de cour* and *comédies-ballets*, many of the latter in collaboration with Molière.

Maintenon, Françoise d'Aubigné, marquise de (1635-1719): married first to Scarron and then to Louis XIV; known for her religious devotion; founded a school for girls at Saint-Cyr, for whom Racine wrote *Esther* and *Athalie*.

Mairet, Jean (1604-86): dramatist, author of 12 tragedies, comedies, tragicomedies and pastorals; strongly opposed to Pierre Corneille in the *Querelle du Cid*.

Malebranche, Nicolas (1638-1715): philosopher, influenced by both Descartes and Augustinian Catholicism; author of *De la recherche de la vérité* (1674-5), *Traité de la nature et de la grâce* (1680), *Traité de morale* (1684) and *Entretiens sur la métaphysique* (1688).

Malherbe, François de (1555-1628): poet; reformed French poetry by his advocacy of coherence and clarity; his reputation was assured by the publication of *Recueil des plus beaux vers de poètes de ce temps* (1627), in which his poetry dominated.

Malleville, Claude de (1597-1647): salon poet.

Mareschal, André (*c.* 1603-*c.* 1650): prose writer and dramatist, perhaps best known for his social satire *La Chrysolite* (1627).

Mascaron, Jules (1634-1703): Oratorian and court preacher.

Massillon, Jean-Baptiste (1663-1742): Oratorian and preacher.

Matthieu, Pierre (1563-1621): historiographer and poet, author of *Tablettes de la vie et de la mort* (1613).

Maynard, François (1582-1646): original member of Académie française, poetic theorist.

Mazarin, Jules, cardinal (1602-61): born in Italy; succeeded Richelieu as first minister in 1642, patron of the arts.

Ménage, Gilles (1613-92): author of *Origines de la langue française* (1650), friend of Mme de Sévigné and Mme de Lafayette, closely involved in the literary salons.

Méré, Antoine Gombaud, chevalier de (1607-84): society man, friend of Pascal, author of *Conversations* (1668) and *Discours* (1677); known mainly as a theorist on *honnêteté*.

Mersenne, Marin (1588-1648): theologian and mathematician, opponent of sceptics and *libertins*.

Mézeray, François Eudes, sieur de (1610-83): historiographer, author of *Abrégé chronologique* (1667).

Mitton, Damien (1618-90): friend of Pascal, who saw him as the epitome of the *honnête homme*; author of *Pensées sur l'honnêteté* (1680).

Molière (Jean-Baptiste Poquelin) (1622-73): great comic play-wright, whose work flourished under the patronage of Louis XIV; author of over 30 plays, including *Les Précieuses ridicules* (1659), *L'Ecole des maris* (1661), *L'Ecole des femmes* (1662), *La Critique de l'Ecole des Femmes* (1663), *L'Impromptu de Versailles* (1663), *Tartuffe* (1664, final version 1669), *Dom Juan* (1665), *Le Misanthrope* (1666), *Amphitryon* (1668), *George Dandin* (1668), *L'Avare* (1668), *Le Bourgeois Gentilhomme* (1670), *Les Femmes savantes* (1672) and *Le Malade imaginaire* (1673).

Molinier, Etienne (*c.* 1600-1650): popular preacher.

Montfleury (Antoine Jacob) (1639-85): comic dramatist.

Montpensier, Anne-Marie-Louise d'Orléans (1627-93): memorialist, first cousin of Louis XIV.

Moreri, Louis (1643-80): priest and author of *Le Grand Dictionnaire historique* (1674).

Motin, Pierre (1566-*c.* 1614): poet.

Naudé, Gabriel (1600-53): librarian and scholar, known for free thought.

Nervèze, Antoine de (*c.* 1570-*c.* 1615): much maligned poet and prose writer.

Nicole, Pierre (1625-95): influential theologian and philosopher, defender of Jansenism; co-author with Antoine Arnauld of the *Logique* (1662), author of *Les Imaginaires* (1664), *Traité de la comédie* (1667), in which he attacks the theatre, and the voluminous *Essais de morale* (1671-8).

Ogier, François (1597-1670); priest, poet and theorist.

Orléans, Gaston d' (1608-60): younger brother of Louis XIII, opponent of Richelieu.

Orléans, Philippe d' (1640-1701): younger brother of Louis XIV.

Pascal, Blaise (1623-62): mathematician, scientist, polemicist and religious apologist; highly influential writer, best known for his satirical *Lettres provinciales* (1656-7), in which he defends the Jansenists and attacks the Jesuits, and for the unfinished *Pensées* (published posthumously in 1670), which constitutes a defense of the Christian religion.

Patin, Guy (1601-72): physician and letter-writer.

Patru, Olivier (1604-81): lexicographer and author of *Les Plaidoyers* (1670).

Pellisson, Paul (1624-93): poet and historian; friend of Fouquet; author of the *Histoire de l'Académie française* (1653).

Perrault, Charles (1628-1703): author of *Contes* (1697), a collection of fairy-tales; sided with the modernists in the debate of *anciens* and *modernes*, and wrote *Parallèle des anciens et des modernes* (1688-97).

Poulain de la Barre, François (1647-1723): disciple of Descartes and proponent of the equality of the sexes.

Poussin, Nicolas (1594-1665): influential painter.

Quinault, Philippe (1635-88): dramatist; author of over 15 comedies, tragicomedies and tragedies; after 1671, wrote libretti for Lully's operas.

Racan, Honorat de Bueil, seigneur de (1589-1670): poet.

Racine, Jean (1639-99): tragic dramatist, author of 12 plays, including *Andromaque* (1667), the comedy *Les Plaideurs* (1668), *Britannicus* (1669), *Bérénice* (1671), *Bajazet* (1672), *Mithridate* (1673), *Iphigénie* (1674), *Phèdre* (1677), *Esther* (1689) and *Athalie* (1691).

Rambouillet, Catherine de Vivonne de Savelli, marquise de (*c.* 1588-1665): aristocrat, who presided over a famous salon in the room known as *la chambre bleue*.

Rapin, René (1621-87): Jesuit teacher and writer on rhetoric.

Regnard, Jean-François (1655-1709): comic playwright.

Régnier, Mathurin (1573-1613): poet and satirist.

Retz, Jean-François-Paul de Gondi, cardinal de (1613-79): churchman, known chiefly for his *Mémoires* (published 1717).

Richelet, César-Pierre (1631-98): lexicographer, creator of the first monolingual French dictionary, the *Dictionnaire français* (1680).

Richelieu, Armand du Plessis, cardinal de (1585-1642): politician and patron of the arts, responsible for the creation of the Académie française.

Roannez, Artus Gouffier, duc de (1627-96): soldier and friend of Pascal; was closely involved in the publication of Pascal's *Pensées* (1670).

Robinet, Charles (*c.* 1608-98): poet and prose writer.

Rotrou, Jean (1609-50): dramatist, best known for his tragedies *Le véritable saint Genest* (1645), *Venceslas* (1647) and *Cosroès* (1648).

Sablé, Madeleine de Souvré, marquise de (1599-1678): author of *Maximes* (published posthumously 1678); ran her own literary salon.

Saint-Amant, Marc-Antoine de Gérard, sieur de (1594-1661): poet.

Saint-Cyran, Jean Duvergier de Hauranne, abbé de (1581-

1643): founding father of Jansenism, friend of Jansenius, author of a number of spiritual works.

Saint-Evremond, Charles de Marguetel de Saint-Denis, sieur de (1613-1703): conversationalist, essayist and occasional poet; many of his works were published as *Oeuvres mêlées* (1705).

Saint-Pavin, Denis Sanguin de (1595-1670): *libertin* poet.

Saint-Simon, Louis de Rouvroy, duc de (1675-1755): significant memoirist, whose writings are largely concerned with the last years of Louis XIV's reign.

Sarasin, Jean-François (1614-54): salon poet.

Scarron, Paul (1610-60): novelist, poet and comic playwright; best known for *Le Roman comique* (1651-7).

Scudéry, Georges de (1601-67): soldier and author; attacked Corneille in his *Observations sur le Cid* (1637); probably collaborated with some of his sister's works.

Scudéry, Madeleine de (1608-1701): prolific prose writer and founder of a literary salon, known as *le samedi*; author of *Les Femmes illustres* (1642), *Le Grand Cyrus* (1649-53) and *Clélie* (1654-60).

Segrais, Jean Regnauld de (1624-1701): poet and literary assistant to the Duchesse de Montpensier, with whom he edited the collection of portraits, *La Galerie des peintures* (1659); friend of Mme de Lafayette.

Séguier, Pierre (1588-1672): chancellor of France and protector of the Académie française.

Senault, Jean-François (1599-1667): Oratorian and philosopher, best known for *De l'usage des passions* (1641); author of *L'Homme criminel* (1644) and *L'Homme chrétien* (1688), both of which are largely derived from the writing of St Augustine.

Sercy, Charles de (dates unknown): bookseller and publisher.

Sévigné, Marie de Rabutin-Chantal, marquise de (1626-96): letter-writer, whose vast correspondence (mostly written to her daughter Mme de Grignan) is justly famous; astute commentator on personal, historical and literary events; friend of Mme de Lafayette, cousin of Bussy-Rabutin.

Silhon, Jean de (1596-1667): theologian and religious apologist; author of *De l'immortalité de l'âme* (1634) and *Les Deux Vérités* (1626).

Simon, Richard (1638-1712): Biblical scholar.

Singlin, Antoine (1607-64): spiritual director at Port-Royal.

Sirmond, Antoine (1591-1643): Jesuit; author of *La Défense de la vertu* (1641).

Somaize, Antoine Baudeau, sieur de (1630-*c.* 1680): author on preciosity, including *Les Véritables précieuses* (1660) and *Le Grand Dictionnaire des Précieuses* (1660-61).

Sorel, Charles (*c.* 1599-1674): novelist, literary critic, historiographer; author of *Nouvelles françaises* (1623), *Francion* (1623) and *Le Berger extravagant* (1627-8).

Tallemant des Réaux, Gédéon (1619-92): memorialist, author of the gossip-dominated *Historiettes* (first published in 1834).

Tavernier, Jean-Baptiste (1605-89): explorer, whose accounts of his journeys were to inspire similar travel literature.

Théophile de Viau (1590-1626): poet and dramatist, known as a *libertin* and imprisoned for alleged impious and obscene poetry.

Tristan L'Hermite (*c.* 1601-55): poet and dramatist, author of the plays *Mariamne* (1636), *La Mort de Sénèque* (1644) and *La Folie du sage* (1645).

Trousset, Alexis (dates unknown): author of *Alphabet de l'imperfection et malice des femmes* (1617).

Turenne, Henri de la Tour, vicomte de (1611-75): outstanding general.

Urfé d', Honoré (1567-1625): novelist and poet; author of the long pastoral romance *L'Astrée* (1607-27).

Vaugelas, Claude Favre de (1585-1650): lexicographer and linguistician; author of the influential *Remarques sur la langue française* (1645); worked on the dictionary of the Académie française until his death.

Vaumorière, Pierre d'Ortigue de (1610-93): author of *L'Art de plaire dans la conversation* (1688).

Villedieu, Marie-Catherine Desjardins, Madame de (*c.* 1640-83): novelist and dramatist; best known for her tragedy *Manlius Torquatus* (1662) and the prose narratives, *Les Désordres de l'amour* (1675) and *Annales galantes* (1670).

Villiers, Pierre, abbé de (1648-1728): Jesuit priest, poet and essayist.

Vincent de Paul, Saint (1581-1660): holy man, whose writings were mostly notes made by his disciples.

Voiture, Vincent (1597-1648): society poet and founding member of the Académie française.

Index